Shining Light Parents Speak

Wisdom and Inspiration from Helping Parents Heal Leaders

by Mark Pitstick MA, DC
and 130 Shining Light Parents

Foreword by Elizabeth Boisson and Gary Schwartz PhD

All profits from this book go to Helping Parents Heal.

ISBN: 9798328134088

Cover and book formatting by Debora Lewis

Cover photograph by David Alison

Editing / production team: Anne-marie Taplin, Dolores Cruz, Allison Alison, and Nancy Hejna

Contents

Contents

Foreword

by Elizabeth Boisson, President and Co-Founder of Helping Parents Heal

It's a pleasure to write a foreword for this book which features remarkable Shining Light Parents who celebrate their children in Spirit and make a difference in the lives of others. This book will help parents to understand that their children are not gone; they are still right here, and they are our biggest cheerleaders. They help us move forward and heal.

Thank you, Dr. Mark Pitstick and Lynn Hollahan, for interviewing many Caring Listeners and Affiliate Leaders in Helping Parents Heal (HPH). I also appreciate the enormous work that Anne-marie Taplin, Dolores Cruz, Allison Alison, and Nancy Hejna have done compiling this book based on those interviews.

Special thanks go to Irene Vouvalides and her vibrant daughter, Carly. Irene is the Vice President and Conference Chair of HPH, and she and Carly are omnipresent in our group. Irene and I communicate at least three times a day! Carly insisted that we needed an HPH conference for parents to get together and share about their children. These incredibly uplifting and healing conferences have sold out since they started in 2018.

In October 2009, as my son Morgan was transitioning to spirit at the Base Camp of Mount Everest in Tibet from severe altitude sickness, I asked his roommate to put his cell phone up to his ear. I told Morgan that we loved him, that we were proud of him, and not to be afraid. As soon as I did, I received the biggest hug from Morgan. Although we were thousands of miles apart, I recognized his amazing bear hug. At that moment, I knew that love never dies and that Morgan would be with me forever.

This 'Shared Death Experience' motivated me to find other parents who were also receiving messages from their children who had passed. However, the existing parent support groups in 2009 did not encourage parents to discuss these signs and validations. I was, therefore, inspired to find others who wanted to share these signs, and I knew I would. I created the Helping Parents Heal Facebook group just one week after Morgan passed.

I am not unique; anyone could have started this group. I feel like a marionette, and that our kids guide me and tell me what to do. They are working hard from the other side to let us know that they are still here, that life is eternal, and that *love lives forever.*

It is essential to find our tribe on this healing journey since family and friends often don't or can't understand. They believe that speaking about our kids will make us sad. Of course, it's the opposite: we always want to talk about our kids! Spending time with like-minded souls is so uplifting and healing.

I have learned that we never leave our kids behind; they walk beside us every step of the way. Morgan and my daughter Chelsea – who passed on very early in life – are just as much a part of my life right now as when they transitioned... perhaps even more so.

Searching for the 'Collateral Beauty' along this journey is essential. Our kids can better connect with us as we raise our vibrations by helping others, eating healthfully, exercising, spending time in nature, expressing gratitude, and doing activities we enjoy. When we sleep, we spend time with our kids on the other side. Although we don't always remember when we wake up, these dream visits make us more peaceful and receptive.

Helping Parents Heal is my extended family, and I am fortunate to know everyone I have met on this healing journey. As Shining Light Parents, we must spread the word that our kids in Spirit are happy, healthy, and whole. Communicating with our children may someday help save the world.

With love and gratitude,

Elizabeth Boisson

www.HelpingParentsHeal.org

Foreword

by Gary E. Schwartz PhD

I am indeed honored to write this foreword for *Shining Light Parents Speak* because Helping Parents Heal (HPH) is a priority for me. I am very impressed by the number of HPH members who are motivated to learn the *clinical, scientific, and experiential evidence* that life continues after the body dies. In addition, I am in awe of some of them who have chosen to awaken more to what we call the 'the big picture of life'.[1] That shift can help them, others, and our planet. Here is just one example of evidence from each category:

1. **Clinical data from near-death experiences** provide strong indications that consciousness is not just a temporary by-product of the brain. Rather, this research shows that consciousness is non-local, primary, and continues after death of the human body.

2. **Scientific research on evidential mediums** was conducted by me at the University of Arizona over 20 years ago as described in my book *The Afterlife Experiments*. Since then, other research has occurred at numerous universities and institutes. As you may have experienced, just one piece of specific, verifiable information relayed this way can become a tipping point for grieving persons to know that the essence of their loved one still exists. Mark Pitstick MA, DC and I wrote *Greater Reality Living* in 2018, in which I shared:

---

1 Katta Mapes MA, MEd, Mark Pitstick MA, DC, and Gary E. Schwartz PhD. *The Big Picture of Life.* Waterside Productions, 2021. This book for young people was adopted from the book *Greater Reality Living* by Mark Pitstick and Gary E. Schwartz.

"Speaking as a scientist, I am now 99.9 percent certain that life continues after bodily death." Based on much research and development since then, I can now more accurately and responsibly say that *life after death has been, beyond reasonable doubt, 'proven' scientifically*.

3. **Experiential evidence** includes perceptions of 'departed' loved ones while in the waking or dream state. These firsthand experiences, termed 'After Death Communications' are quite common and provide further indications that life continues after death.

This collective evidence is great news for all people – including those with one or more children whose earthly forms have perished. My work as a clinical psychologist and with personal grief experiences have shown me how difficult it can be when encountering *what appears to be* the loss of a loved one. However, collective evidence now gathered above shows that it is really more of 'a change' than a loss. That important distinction has made all the difference for many grieving people.

Further, my psychophysiology experiments, which include co-directing the Yale Behavioral Medicine Clinic, and conducting pioneering energy-healing research at the University of Arizona, have all taught me this: **we all have formidable self-restorative and self-actualizing potentials**. For example, we can learn to lower our blood pressure, decrease anxiety, and heighten immune system functioning.

Similarly, *you can learn* to survive, heal, find and share 'silver linings', and create a different but wonderful life after the bodily death of your child. Granted, if he or she recently passed, this may sound impossible. However, many parents have demonstrated it is possible and – in this book – share how.

Information, resources, and support from HPH have helped many people optimally heal and transform. Remarkably, some parents have become *even more empowered and aware* than they were before their child transitioned from earth. From my perspectives as a scientist, clinician, and human being, this is very impressive and inspiring.

At the first two HPH conferences, I shared findings from the field of Soul Science and about The SoulPhone Project. At the 2024 conference, I will update parents about exciting developments in postmaterial communication technology. (The term 'postmaterial' refers to people whose human form has died, but who are still very much alive and active in another realm.[2])

By early 2025, we anticipate that you will be even more informed, comforted, and inspired by the following:

1. Official announcements of scientific proof for life after bodily death

2. Real life demonstrations of postmaterial contact via early SoulSwitch technology.

Current research and development points to the likelihood that you will someday be able to regularly communicate with your postmaterial child via texting, talking, and video-conferencing.

---

2 If you are interested in learning about postmaterial consciousness science, we encourage you to visit the Academy for the Advancement of Postmaterialist Sciences website at https://www.aapsglobal.com/

I hope this great news helps you advance as a Shining Light Parent, improve all aspects of your life, bless others, and make our world a better place.

Gary E. Schwartz PhD

Dr. Schwartz is a former Harvard and Yale professor who recently retired as a professor of psychology, medicine, neurology, psychiatry and surgery from the University of Arizona. In 2024, he was granted Professor Emeritus status by the University of Arizona. A world-renowned author, lecturer, and research scientist, he directed the *Laboratory for Advances in Consciousness & Health* (LACH.Arizona.edu) at the University of Arizona and continues to direct the SoulPhone Project (SoulPhone.org).

Introduction

by Mark Pitstick

Welcome to what may be one of the most important books you'll ever read. ***How it came to be written*** is a fascinating story...

In October 2023, Lynn Hollahan and I began four months of interviewing 130 Affiliate Leaders and Caring Listeners via Zoom. (Lynn, a Shining Light Parent extraordinaire, scheduled the interviews and co-hosted the meetings.) These parents are well along the path of becoming Shining Light Parents. Instead of the term 'bereaved parents', author, teacher, and highly evidential medium Suzanne Giesemann suggested using 'Shining Light Parents'. Why? In her words: "Our children are beautiful shining lights, and as we come to know that they're still right here, we become shining lights for others on the journey!" (#82)

Elizabeth Boisson and Irene Vouvalides, President and Vice-President of Helping Parents Heal (HPH), respectively, enlisted Lynn and I to do this ultra-important but very time-consuming project. I, or Elizabeth for three of the sessions, asked each parent the same six questions:

1. Would you please tell us about your children's life and how they passed on?

2. How did you discover *Helping Parents Heal* (HPH) and how did that help you?

3. How are you now serving others through HPH, and what motivated you to do that?

4. How have you learned to optimally sense your children's living presence?

5. What are three things you've learned that you want to share with other parents?

6. What is your belief about meaning and timing to your children's passing?

Please note that the chapters below are not presented in this order.

From the very start, we could sense what a powerful project this would become. During preparation with six parents before the second set of interviews, Lisa Wilcoxson shared via our group Zoom video call that her sons Michael and Anthony had transitioned from earth. Both of them, she described, were in frequent contact especially via electronic devices. **At that moment**, balloons and fireworks exploded above my head on the Zoom screen. After the 'oohs and ahs' had died down, I asked who made that happen since I didn't. *None of them had done anything to create those images.* After a few moments of stunned silence, Lisa matter-of-factly said, "That's what I was just telling you about my boys! They are always up to something like that."

Since 1972, I've searched for evidence of the afterlife when I started working in hospitals with many adults and children whose earthly forms perished. As a result, my degree of certainty about life continuing after bodily death is very high. **I thought I had heard and seen it all.** However, seeing those balloons and fireworks – when none of us made it happen – took my 'knowing' to another level. I said aloud, "Oh, so that's how these interviews are going to go!" (Unfortunately, we don't have a recording of that amazing event since we hadn't started the actual interviews yet, *but we do have eight witnesses*.)

During the third interview, Allison and David Alison shared how their son Davey often came through loud and clear when they sensed him. David described the importance of being open and accepting to how Davey came through. **At that very moment**, I received an undeniable communication into the right side of my head. It was as though someone had just yelled down from the ceiling.

I actually looked up in that direction and said to David, "Wow, I've got to tell you this. You mentioned listening to 'the voice in my head that was him (Davey) so clearly'. **Just then**, I heard "Mark, you guys need to write a book from these interviews. Capture key phrases and all the wisdom because there's so much there!" Davey recommended the title *Shining Lights Speak* for this book, but we added 'Parents' to it.

I took a deep breath and exhaled, waved my hand as if my face were hot, and stammered: "God! Thank you for his message. Whew! Wow, wow, wow."

Over the last 25 years, I've interviewed many well-known people including Wayne Dyer, Brian Weiss, Raymond Moody, and Caroline Myss. I've hosted two radio shows and given presentations at hundreds of workshops and webinars. Despite all that, I was almost speechless after Davey's apparent communication came through. I now better understand the feelings behind the terms 'mind-boggling', 'gob-smacked', and 'mind-blowing'.

After a few hours of sleep that night, I awakened with an outline for the book seemingly downloaded into my brain. Soon afterwards, I sent an email to some Shining Light Parents. I shared what I just described and asked for volunteers to assemble key statements and stories from the interviews into a book.

Four exemplary Shining Light moms, all with prior writing and editing experience, agreed to help: Anne-marie Taplin leading the project with Nancy Hejna, Dolores Cruz, and Davey's mom Allison. They transcribed words from the videos and identified 'the gold / the best of the best'. (This was a very difficult job since there were so many wonderful stories and statements to choose from.)

The book team then wrote and prepared the first draft. Christiane Robbins and Christine Moncheck handled consent forms created by HPH board member attorney Doryce Norwood. Proofreaders included Jennifer Horner, Barbara Reed, Susan Van Oije, Lin Dobie, David Derby, and Lisa Arnold.

And this book was born!

I deeply thank and appreciate everyone mentioned above and all the Shining Light Parents whose interviews made this book possible! I also thank my beloved partner Andrea Lee who has created such a loving and highly evolved space for the 'kids' to feel welcome and for me to share my highest outreaches. Her waking and dream mediumistic perceptions before, during, and after the interviews repeatedly validated that the children really are alive and in contact!

We hope you feel the sacredness and power of their words as much as we have. May *Shining Light Parents Speak* become *a tipping point for you to deeply know and show that this earthly experience is a totally safe, meaningful, and magnificent adventure amidst eternity.*

Notes:

1. To learn more about selected topics, see free articles indicated by (#___) at SoulProof.com/Articles.

2. I use the term 'postmaterial person' to describe those whose earthly bodies have died and are living in the next phase of life (#31).

Is NOW a Great Time to Transmute Tragedy Into Blessings? I bolded this question to get your attention since it's such a critical one. How you answer it is up to you; we hope this book helps shape your reply into an inspired and resounding YES.

Yes, the bodily death of a child – who passed on at any age and by any means – is one of the toughest challenges that humans encounter. I am not minimizing that at all. However, in 2024, there is much more quality support, information, and resources than ever before. In the recent past, many people suffered greatly because of prevailing beliefs that we now know are not true.

A. In the past, many people BELIEVED...

1. The bodily death of a child is tragic, senseless, and premature.

2. No parent should have to bury their children.

3. God controls the timing of all or most deaths and *His* wisdom must be trusted.

4. Parents must carry a heavy weight for the rest of their earthly lives.

5. Parents may never see their children again if there is no afterlife.

6. Hell may await children who transitioned via suicide, overdose, etc.

B. Now, more people KNOW the following:

1. Your postmaterial child is *an eternal being of consciousness, energy, and life force*. (#15) Parent-child relationships continue in extraordinary ways and do not die. As soulmates (#121), you will likely experience different roles as you explore various time-space slices of life. What's more, postmaterial contact with your child doesn't hurt their progress in the next phase of life. Free of their limiting brain and body, they likely can be in more than one place at the same time. (#75)

2. You didn't really bury or cremate your child, just the no-longer-needed earthly form. Over 99% of who and what they *really are* continues to exist in another dimension / frequency / place. Put another way, their human forms have as little to do with *their real selves* as an outgrown sweater they wore as a child.

3. You and your child are integral, infinite, eternal, and beloved parts of the Creator and Sustainer of all that exists. (#13) As such, their souls took part in the complex decisions about when and how to transition from earth. (#98) Ideally, these decisions were made in alignment with the greater love and wisdom of The Light, angels, and other highly evolved beings. (#73) However, if they weren't, souls have a chance to learn lessons, grow, and be less impulsive in other scenarios.

In A3 above, I italicized the masculine pronoun 'His' for Creator since archaic patriarchal views have created so much unnecessary confusion. Using the feminine pronoun 'Her' corrects many needless quandaries, for example, "Why did God take my child?" (#78). What loving Mother would even imagine acting as cruelly and dictatorially as ancient Roman and Greek-era depictions of a huge long-haired bearded guy in the sky?

4. Some support groups for grieving parents actually have them hold a heavy rock while talking about their child's passing. This symbol reinforces lower energy thinking that your life has to be horrible when, in fact, many parents have shown this doesn't have to be the case. (#108) As you'll see from the interviews in this book, many parents have *chosen* to reclaim a happy life. This is wise for several reasons that will be discussed later.

5. Much scientific, clinical, and firsthand experiential evidence now definitively proves that life continues after bodily death. *There is no doubt about it!* You will have a wonderful reunion with your child when you pass on. What's more, you can enjoy a very real and meaningful relationship with them *right now*. (#1, 60, 115, 9)

6. This concern is needless since there is no eternal place of torment. (#14)

Regarding firsthand experiences, many parents are now more comfortable sharing *signs from their children*. These are immensely comforting and validate that *life and love are forever*. As one parent described: "My son passed on at age 26. On the afternoon of his funeral and memorial, a huge sunset and double rainbow appeared behind our house. I have never seen this before or since. Weeks later, I asked when my son was cremated and found it was the afternoon of the funeral. I believe this was our son going out into the universe."

To learn more about these evidence-based understandings and SHIFT to contemporary perspectives, see articles #2, 4, 15, 16, 20, 27, 68, 72, 76, 100, and 107 at SoulProof.com. Articles #82 and 93 are especially helpful and comprehensive.

Two parents we interviewed summed up all this beautifully. Nancy said: "We began to have signs immediately that Joey is right with us. I was convinced he could not be gone – all that energy cannot just disappear!" Lisa L shared the same view: "There was no way my bundle of energy, intelligence, wit, and loving spirit could vanish. I had to find out where my daughter went and how could I still communicate. I was just driven."

This book will show you how to start optimally healing and transforming. You can come to know, without a doubt, that your child is still very much alive and how you can enjoy a joyful relationship with him or her now. You can learn how to find and share the silver linings – not despite – but because of your child's passing.

If your child recently changed worlds and / or your grief is very raw, these claims may sound like cruel jokes. However, after going through 'the dark night of the soul', many parents have demonstrated it in every aspect of their lives. In time and with help from HPH and others, so can you. The following real-life testimonials show what is possible:

"After my son passed on, I lost my job, and I just couldn't take anymore. Yesterday, I decided that I'm done being on earth. I decided to end my life and actually felt a bit relieved. I just needed to put my stuff in order. Last evening, I decided to attend your HPH class on contacting departed loved ones. I think my son sent me to you because he knows I need the help right now. After sensing him a little more, I decided to stay here and try to make him proud of me."

"I'm writing to let you know how you saved my life. My beautiful son woke up in heaven at the age of 21. My whole world was ripped apart and I struggled to carry on and stay on earth. I found you through HPH and you brought light and hope in my heart. You explained about our loved ones who have dropped their earthly body and don't really die. Because of the amazing work and dedication of you and others at HPH, I now know for sure that my handsome son is right alongside me all the time."

"I wanted to tell you how much your teachings and HPH have helped me since my son's suicide. Your articles about children changing worlds, a just and loving God, and what heaven and hell really are gave me greater hope and insight into the universe.

Chapter 1: Conscious Language

by Mark Pitstick

Helping Parents Heal (HPH) offers support, information, and resources for parents after children have passed on. We encourage you to use the conscious language tips discussed below as well as the resources at the end of this book. HPH leaders are always happy and honored to help so *please don't hesitate to reach out*. Many parents in this organization are on, or have completed, the journey:

FROM hopelessness, guilt, anger, and other lower energies / emotions / ways of being

TO peace, joy, gratitude, enthusiasm, and other higher energies / emotions / ways of being. (#108)

You can make this transition too... especially with all the resources in this book.

In addition to HPH resources, you likely have dear family members, friends, and others who want to assist you. Please let them know what you are going through and how they can help. You also have *your spiritual support team*: angels, guides, and master teachers. (#73) And, everywhere and always available is The Light / Source Energy. (#13) Prayer and meditation are great ways to talk with these highly evolved ones and hear their wise and loving replies. (#89 and 51)

Finally, *you also have yourself*. YOU are much more powerful and resilient than you know. Using all caps with the word 'YOU' denotes that I'm not just talking about your earthly body and brain; that is only a small fraction of who and what you really are. I'm referring to your – *and your child's* – higher self / soul / eternal consciousness / life force.

Again, you and your child are *integral, infinite, and beloved parts* of the Creator and Sustainer of all that exists. You *appear* to be solid, mortal, and separate from others and Source Energy... but none of that is true. In truth, you are timeless beings of energy who are wearing earth-suits during brief earthly experiences. You and your child don't die and your love doesn't end. **The more you deeply know and show this**, the more you can experience his or her very real and near presence. That is a big key to enjoying the greatest life you have envisioned, no matter what is happening to or around you.

I know these concepts are pretty 'deep' but they describe the big picture of life. However, words can fall short when describing ultimate understandings of reality – of what is really going on in life. The resources and conscious language recommended below will help you better know these concepts firsthand. And that, my dear ones, gives you 'the peace that passes all understanding', the wisdom and clarity that all great spiritual teachers have tried to convey.

One 'secret' about how HPH helps so many people so powerfully is sharing these more awakened views. Another is teaching and modeling how to think, speak, and act in higher energy ways. A third, and there are many more, is the immense amount of love and caring that is palpable and helps people remember their true nature.

Here's an example that demonstrates how you can feel... perhaps sooner than you think:

> "I am reading 'Soul Proof' as I sit next to my son's gravesite on the first anniversary of his passing. The last year has been quite

difficult. Today, though, I feel a sense of peace as I sit with him. I learned a term from you that has helped me immensely: 'He just dropped his earthly body.' I now know that what is beneath the ground is just a physical body that he no longer needs. His soul lives on in heaven, he is happy, and I will definitely see him again!"

KNOWING that you'll see your child again is what we wish for all parents and family members. One key to achieving that is using *more accurate words, AKA conscious language*.

Upgrading what you think and say about life on earth, bodily death, and afterlife is an ultra-effective way to optimally heal and transform. We recommend using more accurate words that are *based on scientific, clinical, and / or experiential evidence about the nature of reality*. Put another way, it's very helpful to use words that reflect contemporary understandings instead of erroneous teachings from before the Dark Ages.

To be clear, some ancient religious / spiritual teachings are wise and accurate. However, others were obviously altered by powerful men who sought to gain more wealth and control. When you examine teachings about ultimate matters with an open and loving mind, it's easy to discern which is which. (#16)

Conscious language helps you remember *The Great News* (#19) that includes: (1) life continues after death of the human form; (2) your children are eternal beings who are alive and well in the next phase of life; (3) you will be with them more fully again someday after you pass on; and (4) you can enjoy a different but very meaningful relationship with your children **right now.** As Dr. Gary Schwartz said when we created a glossary for our book *Greater Reality Living*: "We don't want to continue using words that take our minds in the wrong direction."

(Be sure to read article #19 *The Great News* to see the full list of reassuring and inspiring indications of how life is set up. This magnificent news can help you *get through your toughest challenges with style.* You can find silver linings that always accompany adversity and use them to improve every aspect of your life. Then you can begin to help others which will honor your children, create more meaning to their lives, and make them proud of you.)

You can take big steps toward those goals just by thinking and speaking more accurately. *This is not just wishful thinking*, since again, conscious language is based on *solid evidence about the nature of reality*. Some parents have reported feeling noticeably better after shifting their language to better describe how wonderful the big picture of life is. Here's an example...

> "I am writing this right after the funeral of my son whose body died by suicide. Thank you, Mark, you've helped me feel so much better through your teachings. I really do feel peace although I miss my beautiful son so much. We were very close so for me to feel this peaceful now is truly amazing!"

Here's a post on the HelpingParentsHeal.org website about conscious language:

Our Language Is Different!

> We are grateful that you have found us and that our children have brought us together.

Please know that our group is different from other support groups. We believe in a connection with our children in spirit and that they want us to be happy, healthy, and ultimately heal.

We are non-dogmatic, and our parents come from all religions, as well as no religion. We speak of our paths toward connecting with our children as 'healing journeys' instead of 'grieving'. We do not call ourselves 'bereaved' as it is possibly the saddest word in the English dictionary. Instead, we call ourselves Shining Light Parents since the light of our beautiful children shines through us.

We do not say that our children are 'dead' or that we 'lost' them; they are still right here with us and share in everything we do. And they high-five each other when we smile. Plus, the term 'Rest in Peace' is not a part of our vocabulary; our kids are more active, energetic, and alive than we are!

Our children are proud of us and thrilled that we are working together to connect with them and help each other heal. They are our biggest cheerleaders, walking beside us, holding our hands, and leading the way. We appreciate your understanding, and hope you find peace and healing here.

Elizabeth, Irene, and I identified three important concepts that I'll discuss before sharing recommended conscious language terms.

1. You don't have to experience deep grief even though you really love and miss your children.

Contrary to what some grief counselors may say, *you can feel different and even, paradoxically, opposite emotions simultaneously.* For example, you can miss your kids very much, but also feel deep joy and peace because you know 'The Great News' mentioned above. My *Appreciate, Realize, and Transform Technique* (#41) uses deep relaxation and guided imagery to help you focus on those three areas. In this session, your analytical brain – that senses less than 1% of reality – becomes more quiet so you can remember and perceive the other 99+%.

You can deeply miss and love your children AND – at the same time – make conscious choices to feel happy and fulfilled for several reasons:

A. To be more on the same wavelength as your children and thus better communicate with them. They are, or soon will be, on a frequency characterized by high levels of love, peace, joy, enthusiasm, and much more. As such, *it's difficult to send and receive messages to your children if you are stuck in lower energy emotions* such as anger, guilt, denial, etc. This issue isn't a criticism of anyone who is temporarily stuck at that level. Choosing – on a daily basis – higher energy thoughts, words, and ways of being isn't easy... but it's possible. (#108)

B. To honor your children who are, quite possibly, more evolved souls who only needed to be on earth for a short while. You can show gratitude for parenting such advanced ones – even if only briefly – by creating more meaning in their life and passing.

C. You and your family deserve to be happy and healthy and the world needs your greatest gifts. Despite appearances to the contrary, God wasn't asleep at the wheel, and the passing of your children was not your fault. There is a loving, wise, and fair rhythm to life that exceeds your wildest imaginations. Your limited brain may only partially fathom that, but your heart and soul know it's true. Assuming that perspective helps you see and utilize the silver linings more quickly and powerfully.

2. Toxic Positivity

This term refers to trite statements by well-meaning family, friends, ministers, and health care providers. With the pronoun 'they' referring to your children who have changed worlds, examples include: "They're in a better place." "They are in God's hands." "May they rest in peace (RIP)". "God wanted your children to be with Him." These platitudes don't satisfy many parents who think for themselves, so I'll address each one:

A. *"They're in a better place"* implies, whether intentionally or not, that your child's earthly life wasn't that good in one or more ways. In addition, if parents are concerned about a less-than-heavenly outcome for their children, this statement may stir up fears. (#14) Finally, although your children are in a better place – realms characterized by love and light – parents certainly aren't in a better place, at least not initially. Thus, this statement can make deeply grieving parents feel even worse.

B. *"They are in God's hands"* misses the fact, based upon much clinical evidence, that we each are always integral parts of The Divine. Your children may now realize that more deeply while perceiving more of reality than their limited human brains allowed. However, this statement minimizes or disregards how parents feel when they can't physically see, hear, touch, and smell their beloved children. Parents understandably want their children to be in their hands, not God's.

C. *"May they rest in peace"* isn't ideal for several reasons. That phrase, or its acronym 'RIP', has often been inscribed on grave-side monuments. To those without evidence-based views, that phrase may imply that children's souls are still in the grave resting for who knows how long. On the contrary, much clinical and scientific evidence demonstrates an uninterrupted transition of consciousness after the earthly body dies. Finally, RIP ignores multiple sources of evidence that your children are actively engaged in their new slice of life.

D. *"God wanted your children to be with Him"* is easily the most bizarre. Those words are supposed to be comforting, but numerous parents consider them abhorrent. This phrase portrays the Creator as a needy big guy in the sky who arbitrarily and selfishly decides who dies and when. That statement also neglects the evidence that *souls change worlds based on many factors*. (Ideally, those soul-based decisions align with higher guidance.)

To be fair, many people don't know what to say when children pass on. Those who aren't yet awakened to the big picture of life may consider the bodily death of children to be the worst nightmare imaginable. (I'm not at all saying it's easy, but many parents have shown that life can be just as good, or even better, afterward.)

The bodily death of children may magnify conscious or unconscious fears of that happening to your family and friends. It may also stir up worries about their own passing and what might happen afterward. Those on the journey of becoming

Shining Light Parents can teach others that — although it may feel like it at first — it's not the end of the world when children move into the next stage of life. From an enlightened perspective, the timing and meaning of children's bodily deaths are apparent. (Interviews with HPH Affiliate Leaders and Caring Listeners make this quite clear. See #4 under Recommended Action Steps below.)

Please educate others about what you need and want, and how that changes over time. For example, some family and friends are uncomfortable talking about children who passed on and may not even say their names. This reluctance is ironic because *many parents want to talk about their children*. They want to tell and hear stories, say their names, and keep their kids alive in their hearts and minds. Tell your dear ones about this so they better understand.

3. Spiritual By-Passing

This term refers to the judgment that parents are 'skipping the grieving process' by moving too quickly toward helping others. In other words, some people think you should lay in bed or sit around severely mourning for a long time after your children pass on. From my clinical work, I suspect this difference in perspective has to do with several factors:

A. The degree of support from earthly and higher-energy sources that parents have

B. How much parents know and have internalized the evidence that definitively proves life continues after death

C. Whether early religious teachings were wise and loving, or misinformed and fear- based

D. To what degree parents 'buy into' societal beliefs versus trusting their inner wisdom

E. How advanced the parents' energy / consciousness / soul is.

It's almost comical that exemplary Shining Light Parents like Elizabeth Boisson have been accused of 'spiritual by-passing'. Within a week of her son Morgan's transition, Elizabeth started searching for better ways to help other grieving parents. Based on all my training and experience, she and others who seek 'the high road' are way-showers with evolved responses.

If others make outdated or inaccurate statements, please don't take it personally. Assume that they are trying to help, even though their words may hurt. Realize that their concepts are remnants of an era when most people didn't realize that **bodily death is just a comma, not a period, in life's never-ending but often-changing story.**

These three concepts, and the five limiting words below, are not meant to be an exhaustive list. We hope our discussion of these will help you to: (1) spot other offending / false statements, (2) not be negatively triggered by them, and (3) find more accurate terms.

You can upgrade your vocabulary to reflect your new beliefs and inner knowing. Your words shape your beliefs which, in turn, determine your thoughts and actions. This shift isn't just a meaningless academic exercise in semantics. *The more you can accurately think and speak about the nature of reality,* **the more you can know and show 'The Great News'** in every aspect of your life. We especially encourage using more conscious language in place of the following words:

1. Bereaved

This word conveys *deep grieving* that may last for a long time or never end. Many Shining Light Parents have demonstrated that this does not have to be the case. As Elizabeth Boisson beautifully explains: **"There is a much softer and soulful way to grieve versus how it's usually done."** That is such a powerful and true statement; we hope you print and post it where you'll see it often.

The term 'grieving parent' is an improvement since it doesn't convey as much despair and hopelessness as 'bereaved'. However, we favor using the term *Shining Light Parent.* Regarding the need for this term, Irene Vouvalides wrote: "I don't want to be known as *a bereaved parent*. To me, that is the saddest word in the dictionary, and I cringe every time I hear it. I'm a Shining Light Parent. There is a huge difference in energy when you say one versus the other."

As mentioned in the Introduction to this book, HPH has adopted this term to capture *the higher energy way* of viewing the death of your children's bodies. (Notice the specific language here: the entirety of who and what your children ARE didn't die – just the earthly shells they used for a while perished. The word 'just' may seem cruel, but it's justified since *over 99% of who and what your children really **are** still exists*.)

Here's one way to look at it. If you've flown much, you know that the sun always shines in your area during daylight hours. However, depending on cloud formations, you may not be able to see it much or at all from the ground. (Ironically, I am writing this during a total solar eclipse in our area. That's a rare example of why the sun can't be seen.)

Similarly, whether they feel that way yet or not, ***all grieving parents are Shining Light Parents right now*** because:

A. They and their children are eternal beings of consciousness, energy, and light.

B. They and their children are integral parts of Source Energy / Creator.

C. They can find silver linings and bless others with them.

D. It helps their postmaterial children shine even more brightly.

2. Committed suicide

The word 'committed' is usually used in negative contexts, for example, "He committed a crime." The phrase also supports archaic and false beliefs that suicide is a one-way ticket to hell – as if a loving Creator would even imagine such a place. (#4) Similarly, we reject the term "He killed himself" since the soul / life force is indestructible. We recommend using other terms, for example "She passed on by suicide" or "He ended his earthly experience via suicide".

3. Die and death

These words are heavily anchored to inaccurate beliefs that your 'departed' loved ones have ceased to exist, are decomposing in the ground, have been reduced to ashes, or are very far away. Other erroneous notions reinforced by these words are that you may never see them again, or you cannot communicate with them until the death of your human form.

Much contemporary evidence indicates that none of the above are true. As such, we instead recommend terms such as 'passed on', 'changed worlds', 'graduated from earth-school', and 'transitioned to the next phase of life'. We also encourage you to use specific modifiers with 'die / death', such as 'death of her human form', 'his body died', 'death of her human body,' 'his human form died', 'death of her earthly body' or 'his earth-suit died'.

4. Lost

This word doesn't accurately describe what happens when your children transition from earth. Yes, their earthly forms perished, but you didn't lose them. And they are not 'lost' – they are more 'found' than we are. When parents say, "We lost our daughter", it reinforces old and misinformed beliefs that bodily death is the end of life. You can enjoy different but highly meaningful relationships and contacts with them now.

Alternative terms that better capture the eternal nature of life and love include "Our son changed worlds" and "Our daughter graduated from earth-school." "Our children moved into the next realm."

5. Passed away

This term can be interpreted as meaning 'passed into nothingness'. As you now know, much evidence indicates this is definitely not true.

We recommend using 'passed on' or simply 'passed', or other options listed under 'Die and death'.

Adopting conscious language and upgrading the way you think and speak requires some work. New terms, although more accurate, may initially seem cumbersome. However, parents have shared that the effort helps them better remember the big picture of life.

Read on for uplifting and energizing words from these Shining Light Parents. *Please pace yourself* to get the most out of this book since their statements are often very 'deep' and may be emotional for you to read.

Chapter 2: Sensing Your Child's Presence

by Dolores Cruz

Our children have graduated from earth-school, but they are not far away. They are in a different realm, dimension, or vibrational reality that many of us cannot detect with our five senses. However, a sixth sense and other ways to perceive them can come into play. This chapter answers the question: *How have you learned to optimally sense your children's living presence?*

Members of Helping Parents Heal have shared how their kids communicate through a vast array of signs: a bird, license plate, song on the radio, touch, or whisper. These connections are easily dismissed by people who have no need for them and consider them to be mere coincidences. But those of us who have had these pleasantly surprising signs and synchronicities have no doubt they are from our children. There is an unexplainable resonance that accompanies these validations. When you know, you know.

The following accounts of 130 Affiliate Leaders and Caring Listeners interviewed are just a small sampling of those told by many thousands of members of Helping Parents Heal. This book offers an excellent representation of the continued connections we have with our children. They are always with us because love never dies and the relationship continues. To learn more about the life and passing of these children, see 'Tribute to Participating Parents and Children' at the end of the book.

The Natural World

"She said to me once, 'I'm going to send you a rainbow.'
There were no clouds in the sky, but by the time I got
home – maybe three minutes later — my husband said:
'There's a rainbow outside, but it's not raining!'"

— Marie, Sienna's mom

A very common sign from our loved ones is through the natural world: birds, butterflies, feathers, clouds, rainbows, and heart-shaped rocks, to name a few. It's not that our children become the bird or butterfly; rather, they are able to somehow influence nature signs to show up for us at just the right time. Our children are also able to nudge us to look out the window at the right moment to see the rainbow or the heart-shaped cloud or rock.

Chris R's son Sean communicated with his parents right away after his transition from earth at age 23. "On the night we decided to discontinue Sean's life support, we left the hospital and sat out on a patio. As the sun went down, illuminated over the hospital, the sky looked just like a giant pair of angel wings. We always called him our Angel Boy and his middle name was Gabriel."

Speaking about his son Kevin who changed worlds at age 19, **Tom M** says with amazement: "One time he even created a full, ripe yellow lemon on a lemon tree within a couple of weeks. It usually takes four to twelve months for a lemon to sprout and mature!"

Amy gets signs from her son Chris who crossed over at age 21. "He still shows signs. He comes more with animals: a bird will follow me while I'm walking. Or a squirrel will run up, look at me and not move, turn around and look at me again for another minute or so, and then take off."

Christina, who passed on at age 17, sent her mom **Tava** a gift that put her belief in motion. "Christina was a math and science person and so the way she did things, she would put things in my life that were kind of strange and unusual and had me take note of them and then they would all come together in a moment. The first time this happened was a few months after she transitioned. It all came at a moment where I felt the peace that passes all understanding. I was sort of a Christian — I went to church a few times a year, but I was not already into spirituality."

Tava continues, "So, when I fell on the ground outside my front door and this butterfly swirled around my head twice, I just put my hand up and said 'Christina thank you, oh my gosh, you're here!' Once that happened, it allowed me to accept every little thing that she sends. The biggest aha moments were when my body chemistry actually changed after she came through me. I felt this incredible sense of love and peace that I had never experienced before."

Deb N knows that it helps to keep in communication with her son Dean who changed worlds at age 24. "I love getting signs from Dean and I always thank him. His ability to provide them is just incredible. On Thanksgiving Day, I was out in my mother-in-law's backyard overlooking the Pacific and this hummingbird was flying around as the sun was setting. I said, 'Dean, it would be really nice if you could help me out here and let me take a picture of that hummingbird in front of the sunset.' The little hummingbird landed on top of a bush lined up with the sun and sat there for 10 minutes as the sun set. That's the kind of thing that he's really responsive to. I just believe it.

It's a choice, and it takes time to get there. But I know he's here and I recognize it, ask him for signs, and he shows up with them."

Linda O, David's mom, finds joy in the signs he brings. "Signs include seeing his face in the clouds, rainbows, and having butterflies suddenly land on me. It just fills my heart with love." David crossed over at age 28.

Anni heard from her son Anthony very quickly after he changed worlds. "The day after he transitioned from earth, I opened my curtains and there was a massive heron on the roof opposite. I live in suburbia, it's not as if it's in a woodland. Then there were buzzards. Some people used to call me the crazy bird lady! Just knowing that our children still exist, that they're still here, is an absolute lifeline."

Nicolas sent his parents **Conrado** and **Paola** a surprise visitor. His dad tells us: "This has been mind-blowing from day one when we were in our house crying because this guy from school called us up. They wanted a photo of Nicolas wearing the Torrey Pines colors, and the mascot is the falcon. I was crying upstairs, and Paola came upstairs to ask, 'What's the matter? What's the matter?' I replied, 'I'm looking for a photograph with Nicolas wearing falcon colors.' She started crying too. But while going through photographs, a falcon landed within 10 feet of our fence and just looked at us. We both stopped crying and just stared at it. That was the beginning of our journey."

Angela L's son Ethan was 18 when he moved into the next phase of life. "Often, Ethan gives us assurance and validation in the kookaburra, an Australian native bird with a loud laugh call. The words and tune of an old Australian song about the kookaburra were coming to us all the time."

Sam was 19 when he crossed over. His mom **Kerry** tells us: "Sam has always been prolific with feathers. That may sound whimsical, but it's where you find the feathers and how they affect you. It's not every feather, it's when it's on a special occasion. We will find them in the strangest places like on my husband's desk. Or when I arrived in London at Paddington Station, I could see this thing floating down above the enclosed station. It was two feathers entwined… I felt it was signifying Sam and me!"

Barb says her son Jordan is amazing. "I sit outside and we can ask for a falling star and he will provide it. My husband and I were camping and it was super cold. We wanted to go inside quickly so we gave him a countdown. By the time we were down to 4 there went the shooting star right where we said it was going to be." Jordan passed on at age 25.

Sienna was 11 when she suddenly changed worlds. Her mom **Marie** says: "Sienna was very connected to nature, and I felt very early on a sense of that connectedness. I would often feel and hear messages from her. That has now morphed into dreams and hearing in my mind one-liner sentences that come to be evidential."

Merle found her connection with her son Chris to be very much like his personality. "Chris was loud. One of our loud birds in Australia is the Black Cockatoo. It screeches, and he had a passion for black cockatoos; he just loved them. So when I hear one fly over and screech, I know that's Chris telling me, 'Hey Mum, I'm here, I'm just on my way past.' I don't necessarily always sense his presence, but I know he's here. I don't have any doubt about that and I look for his signs. I look for number plates, birds, feathers, coins and I get subliminal messages. One day as I was leaving work, he said: 'Look up Mum!' and there was a big heart in a cloud." Chris was 34 when he graduated from earth-school.

"One of the first ones was a tiny frog," says **Babette**, mom to Daniel who transitioned from earth at age 25. "Daniel loved frogs and since his passing we've received hundreds of frogs. One time I was desperate for a sign and asked him for a frog, even though it wasn't the right season for them. When I got up and opened a cabinet in the house, a frog jumped out and landed on my leg! It's just been magical."

Pamela's daughter Michele transitioned in 2018 when she was 20 years old. "One morning I woke up and went into her bedroom to find she had passed to the spirit world in her sleep. It was a complete shock. After the police and everyone left, I sat outside and this beetle landed by my feet. It had flipped upside down and was doing this thing where it's trying to turn itself back over. It was doing this on and on and it became comical, and it made me think of my daughter because that is her personality. She would do something silly to try to cheer me up. I was raised Methodist and had become very skeptical about religion, God, the afterlife, and mediums. But something about this little beetle made me think that Michelle was there trying to cheer me up."

Merilene's son Kevin made his transition from earth after a three-and-a-half-year illness. "I wish I could say I could hear and see him as clearly as some other people do, but I do talk to him all the time. I get signs and I feel the love he has for his family will never go away. His love is the only truth. I find coins, shells in the shape of a heart, and birds seem like they are talking to me."

Mary D's daughter Lea was 32 years old when she left this world and graduated to the next. Mary explains that she was able to be with Lea throughout her cancer journey since the family only lived fifteen minutes away. "We tried different approaches: first holistic, then traditional, but everything stopped working after two years. Hospice was called to the house and was there for around two weeks until Lea passed. On that morning, the hospice chaplain arrived and I told her, 'I'm just going to go home and take a quick shower. I'll be right back.' She looked at me and said, 'Don't be long.'"

Mary continues, "I had never been around death or dying and really didn't know much at the time. I went home and took a shower. Then I went outside and, as I looked at my garden and pool, saw a female cardinal skim the surface of the water. It caught my gaze. It felt like time stopped. Seconds later a phone call came and I didn't need to answer it. I just knew. I went to her and everybody was already there. I saw that Lea had a smile on her face. It made me laugh because it was such a surprise. At first, I thought she left that smile for me, but I think it was really what she saw about the wonder and the beauty on the other side."

Electronics and Lights

"In the first month and a half after he passed, Chris was sending messages like crazy, but I wasn't getting it. I knew something was happening because the bathroom lights would flicker every night. I'd go in there and they were flickering; I'd leave the bathroom, and they stopped flickering. Then I'd get in bed and the bedside light would flicker. I was in such a fog that I thought there was

something wrong with the electricity in the house. Finally,
I met someone who said, 'Oh, that's Chris.'"

— Amy D, Chris's mom

Our children try to get our attention in any way they can including through lights, phones, and home electronics. In these cases, parents often try to figure out if there is a logical reason for these incidents. But when there isn't, they conclude it has to be their child getting their attention and saying hello because there is no other explanation for how these things can happen.

One way **Michelle T**'s daughter Jordan stays in touch is by phone. "She has sent me text messages. I got a message just last week from her in the Notes app on my iPhone. So she's pretty powerful and she is loving her life."

Judi's niece, Carly, also communicates with her through the phone. "Shortly after Carly's transition to spirit I came home from Irene's house exhausted. At about 11 o'clock at night, I was alone and texted Carly on my phone: 'Please help me help your mom. I don't know what to do.' Then I fell asleep but there was a message when I woke up: 'Heaven looks a lot like the mall.' I knew it was Carly, so we started this communication." Carly went Home at age 24.

Margaret felt she had an after death communication with her child. "On the night of the accident, there was a phone call; 'Unknown Caller' came up for the caller ID. When I picked up the phone, there was no one speaking – just static. This happened at 3:30 in the morning. Looking at the police report, I realized my son had reached out to me at the time of his accident."

"Josh is an amazing communicator" says **Andy** about his son who moved into the next realm at age 20. "In fact, on the day of his viewing, he messed with the audio-visual system at the funeral hall. He loved to be behind the camera and never wanted to be in front of it. So he messed with the AV. It worked before his viewing and it worked after, just not during! He also messed with the lights in the room."

Cathy sensed her son Ross for the first time on his birthday just five days after he passed on. "I was looking at pictures of his prior birthdays as a little kid and the light overhead kept flashing on and off. I thought there was something wrong with the light switch. Then I went back to looking at the pictures and the lights started flashing again. Then it dawned on me; this is Ross. He's acknowledging that I'm looking at his pictures. At that time somebody knocked on our door to bring me a casserole. She was expecting a bereaved parent sobbing. I said, 'Oh my God! I got a sign from Ross!' I was all excited, and she probably thought I had absolutely lost my mind."

"I didn't believe in survival of consciousness after death," remarks **Ramona**, whose daughter Mia was one month old when she moved into the next realm. "But Mia sure tried from the first day to communicate. When we came home from the funeral – and, of course, imagine the state I was in – we were eating at the table with my parents, Mia's godparents, my husband, and my two other daughters. There was a printer in the room which was definitely turned off. Suddenly, it turned on by itself and printed a blank page. This is something that even my husband, who is a techie, can't explain to this day. When it's turned off, it's turned off."

"Lights are a huge sign from my son," says **Lisa H** whose son Shayne changed worlds at age 16. "My husband is a video designer and

41

there were many screens to contend with when Shayne was here. Shortly after Shayne passed, my husband and I witnessed a sequence of rainbows spontaneously going across a screen while watching a game my husband had created just for Shayne. But it was never coded that way! It was my son manipulating it and coming through to us. My husband has since developed a way for Shayne and his own daughter to communicate with us using a light show in his room."

Louise's daughter Jillian uses her sense of humor to get her mom's attention. "Jillian is a great communicator. She's not dead. Her body is, but she's not. I felt her from day one and she's never gone away. She sends me winks that are just over the top and fit with her sense of humor. Besides sending me coins and monarch butterflies, which we now raise in her honor, she hijacked my mom's TV at the nursing home that played an inappropriate show which she thought was hilarious. The nursing staff couldn't turn it off and had to throw a blanket over the TV!" Jillian crossed over at age 19.

McKellar crossed over at age 19. His mom **Amy** tells us, "He gave me the most amazing gift by July 2nd. I woke up and was able to see an entire non-physical astral plane in my room for about an hour. I could see energy, this loving and beautiful healing light. I knew for a fact that he was still existing, that his energy was still around. It didn't take away the despair and the torment of him not living in the physical, but I knew he was still alive so it gave me hope. It made me start the journey of: 'OK, we're going to find him, we're going to keep connecting.'"

Mary's daughter Katherine made her transition from earth at age 29. "Katherine was on life support for five days. We made the decision to take her off because they gave us no hope of a recovery. She and I had seen psychic mediums before and I knew that it was possible for us to still communicate after she transitioned. So when we disconnected her body, I told her that I wanted to hear from her – I wanted a relationship and communication. That night I went home and laid down on the bed. All of a sudden, there were these purple lights shimmering and moving all around and one of them was Katherine. It was her face in repose and everything was light except for her face. It lasted for a while and gradually they all left. I really felt like this was Katherine saying 'Hey, I'll go with you guys, but first I have to say goodbye to my mom, just let her know that I'm here.'"

Dreams

"I have learned that I can continue to communicate with Carly, that I still have a relationship with her. I talk to her all of the time and encourage her to send me signs which I get in the forms of songs, rainbows, and dream visits. In one of my dream visits I asked her, 'Are you with me?' She said, 'I'm always with you but I'm busy, I have a life here. If you call on me I'll be there but I have things to do.'"

— Irene, Carly's mom

If you've ever had a very vivid and comforting dream about your loved one, it may have been more than just a dream. Dream visits are a common way for our children and other loved ones in spirit to connect with us to send us a message or let us know they are doing very well. Parents describe these dreams as being so real that they could feel their child's hug or smell their hair. They wake up feeling like they have been with their child.

David D's daughter Ginger crossed over at age 20. "My connection is still a work in progress, but I've had moments of vivid communication with my daughter. An example is when I saw Ginger in a dream. She was standing in my kitchen and we were talking. I'm color blind and only see about four different colors but she was in a rainbow. I was seeing colors that I've never experienced in my waking life. I said to her, 'But Ginger, you're dead.' She got this big grin on her face and said, 'Not anymore.'"

Beverly says her son Mason, who made his transition from earth at age 19, is pretty active. "Shortly after he transitioned, I had a visitation dream where he just let me know that he was okay, healthy and healed. It was very strong. When you have very strong signs, trust your intuition. You'll know if it's something more than wishful thinking. Parents should trust that the love and the bond with their child is eternal; it doesn't end when their physical body transitions."

Jeff C tells us that his son Austin, who passed on at age 24, has been in his dreams several times. "But I had one distinct dream visit that I still can't describe in words. The only way I tell people is I could just feel it, and I knew it was him. I was able to hug him and feel him. It was a very powerful experience."

"A few days after Grace died, I had my very first visitation dream, reports mom **Michelle J**. "At that time, I didn't know that a visitation dream was a thing. In the dream, she was in a forested area in Australia, and I was walking along this path. She was in front of me, dancing around and super happy. She turned around, held out her hand, and said: 'Come with me, Mum.' I remember waking up in the middle of the night, and *knew* I had been with her. I knew it wasn't just a dream. I also knew that when she said, 'Come with me, Mum', it wasn't an invitation for me to die, but rather an invitation to connect with her, to stay connected, and to find her. We were going to have an ongoing journey." Grace moved into the next phase of life at age 19.

Beth and Rick O have two children who changed worlds at the same time. Josh passed at age nine and Jessica at age seven. Beth shares: "When Jess and Josh died, they started coming to me in dreams instantly and talking to me. I've always kept a dream journal. They help me and give me great advice. They helped us have more children when it was time. I don't dream about them as much now; I just feel them more. I can always tell when they're present."

Linda R says that when her 36-year-old son Chris changed worlds, "I was asleep and my late husband appeared to me in a dream, telling me he will be there to meet our son. At the time it didn't make sense to me until I found out about Chris. With each person who has passed on, they visit me in dreams."

"I have learned that I can continue to communicate with Carly, that I still have a relationship with her," says Carly's mom **Irene**. "She doesn't have a body any longer but I will always be her mother. Just a week after her birthday, I had a dream visit where I was at the HPH conference and couldn't get into my room. I had to call maintenance to come and remove the lock to my room. When I got inside, Carly was there with a bunch of girls. There were clothes piled everywhere and they were putting makeup on, chatting, and having fun. I said, 'Are you really here?' and she said, 'Well of course we're here!'"

Irene continues, "I said, 'Can you help me pick something out to wear for the conference?' She told me to worry about that myself because she was thinking the same thing! I thought *oh typical Carly* and I left. When I left and shut the door I realized that all of the girls in the room with her were all girls in Spirit. The next day I got a pair of jeans by mail and when I put them on I thought, *Wow, these jeans are great, they're stretchy, they look good.* I ripped the tag off and looked... the jeans were called The Carly! She was too busy to help me dress for the conference but she made sure that pair of jeans arrived in time." Carly transitioned from earth at age 24.

Anne-marie's son Harry was 19 when he changed worlds. "Harry comes to me mostly through either dreams or visitations. Visitations are hyper-real, memorable, and usually filled with emotional connection so they're unmistakable for me in terms of how different they are to dreams. The dreams I have, I feel like Harry is entering them from a dimension where he can reach me in my dream state. They're probably more like 'nudges' where he inserts himself into a narrative that my brain is creating. Several encounters have been incredibly profound: most are a meeting of souls with high emotional content, and also more instructional-type dreams."

Songs and the Radio

"I got in the Uber and this young kid is playing 80's music. And I'm thinking, 'Why is he playing 80's music?' The next thing I hear is, 'Hi, we're your DJs Nicole and Ryan.'"
— Marla, mom to Shane, Nicole, and Ryan

A song that comes on the radio with just the right message... this is not merely a coincidence, but another creative way our children have found to communicate with us. They are able to nudge us to turn on the radio or change the station at just the right time. Our kids can also put songs into our heads that provide exactly what we need to hear. When they do this, they confirm that they are always around.

Barb says, "Jordan gives me songs on the radio that just happen to answer the questions I was thinking. Or the stereo turns on and there's an appropriate song."

Aleia and her mom **Kelley** listen to music together. "Aleia loves playing music. She's a musician, a vocalist, and plays the guitar. So I'll throw on my Spotify playlist and say, 'Do you want to DJ?' I'll hit 'shuffle' and songs that just make sense will come up."

Wendy's son Hugh made his transition from earth at age 20. "I decided to go to a medium and took her course. She taught us a meditation that I just love. One day during the meditation the word 'Diplo' popped in and I thought, 'What the heck word is that?' I wrote it down and, a week later, was driving and heard a song on the radio that I really liked. I looked at the digital display: the artist was Diplo and the song was 'Don't Forget My Love.' I just pulled over and cried with joy."

Scott sent his mom **Sara R** a two-for-one. "Probably one of the strongest ways early on was songs. I'd walk into a store and hear the song 'Sarah Smile', or something like that. I knew it was coming right to me. I think it was on Scott's ninth anniversary, my husband and I were eating lunch at a restaurant. The music system was playing two songs at the same time which was so annoying. But one of the songs was 'Sarah Smile' and right on top of it was 'Angel' by Sarah McLachlan. That was Scott letting me know he's with me. Now I hear him all the time day and night. He's my guide."

Dolores's son Eric, who graduated from earth-school at age 24, was a drummer in a band. "We connect through music. When I'm in the car listening to music, Eric is right there with me. When I hear the drums, I talk with him about the drums and it very much feels like that's Eric playing the drums. I really feel that. There's just no doubt he's with me."

Chris V shares, "One of my favorite signs from Daniel was while driving home from the cemetery where his body is buried. The radio dial changed without anyone touching it and started playing 'Stairway to Heaven.'"

Feeling, Seeing, and Hearing

"I felt a touch on the end of my nose. I said his name and there was this surge of energy in my body. When it reached my heart, it was just pure divine love."

— Terri, Rick's mom

Many parents have an awareness of their child's presence through their senses. Some say they have seen their child objectively right in front of them, even for just a moment. They may hear their child's voice call them or whisper "I love you" in their ear. And many feel their child's physical touch: a warm surge of energy, kiss on the cheek, sweet hug, or silly poke on the arm while falling asleep. These glimpses may not happen very often, but even the memory of that one time can create smiles for a lifetime.

Paige's son Brian changed worlds at age 23. She feels his energy, for example, "I was in meditation just today and felt him here (touches right side of her head) and my spirit guide here (touches the left side of her head). I literally felt Brian's energy move to the back and I said: 'Oh, Brian's in the background, he's sitting in the back.' Then I felt his energy move to the front because he had something to say. I share that with you because – if I didn't understand energy and have this sensitivity – I don't think I'd be at the place I am today. The other sign I've received is what I call 'The Brian Hug'. He literally sends his energy through the crown of my head to fill my entire body to the point where it is vibrating and shaking. It's the most special feeling. I don't get those very often but, when I do, I know he's sending me every ounce of his love. It's such a beautiful thing."

"Alex was all about Christmas," relates his mom **Kaylene.** "He is no elf on the shelf, he needs to be included. So I thought: I've got to go shopping and put up a little Christmas tree on the piano. That was the way I was going to do Christmas. I went into this shop and, all of a sudden, could feel this sensation on my head that I hadn't felt before. I dismissed it but then it came again and I thought: 'I have to pay attention'. It became like a game of hot and cold: I turned left and couldn't feel it, turned right and could feel it, then up and down. After about five minutes of paying attention, I found my little Christmas tree tucked behind something else on the ground. No one would have seen it and it was the perfect thing. I said, 'Thank you, Alex. I finally understand'. I knew he was here; it was the greatest gift." Alex was 14 when he returned Home.

Kathy's sons, Aiden and Conor, have both transitioned into the next world. "I've learned a whole lot. I didn't know what I was experiencing in the beginning, but now I have words to put to it. I feel that everybody has an easier way through 'the clairs', for example, clairsentience means 'clear feeling'. Immediately after Aiden passed I felt him touching my face. It made sense because that was what he had done while he was here physically. I can feel emotions and a shift in a room if somebody is in a bad mood. The boys know that. They know so much more than I know."

Lee was 30 when he moved on from earth. His mom **Rosanne** reports, "I feel him quite a bit, actually. I feel tingles on the left side of my head – like bugs crawling around – and then I know that he's present with me."

Ty, Shayna's mom, says: "I get a warmth, even in a cool room – really warm. I see the color purple and that was Shayna's favorite color so I know she's right there with me." Shayna passed on when she was 15.

"Right from the word go I sensed David," says **Linda O**, whose son changed worlds at age 28. "But I was so deep in my grief in the initial months. After six months, though, I started to explore that. I was aware of him stroking my head and felt tingling sensations on my face. It was like my crown chakra and brow chakra were 'on fire.'"

Tammy's son Chris kisses her. "When I meditated, I always felt this tingling on top of my head, and I thought I was feeling Spirit. It's really just a kind of learning. Every time he left, he would kiss me on top of my head and tell me he loved me. I realized he's kissing me on top of my head. So that's how I know when I'm connected with him."

After Rick transitioned from earth at age 23, his mom **Terri** had quite a profound experience. "I was trying to go to sleep and was talking to Rick in my mind. I had read that our children keep their memories so I was saying: 'I know it was difficult at times with the addiction, but I hope you have good memories'. I rolled over and then I felt this touch on the end of my nose. I said his name and there was this surge of energy that flowed through every part of my body. I knew it was the love I share with Rick. I only felt that once, but once is enough."

"Zack will sit on my bed with me while I meditate and I can feel his vibration." says his mom **Renee**. "He makes his presence known everywhere. I was driving in his truck two weeks after he passed on and the steering wheel moved by itself to put me in another lane. I never told a soul, thinking no one would believe me. A medium told me soon after that my son prevented me from being in an accident that day." Zack crossed over at age 24.

Joyce has two daughters in spirit: Holly who passed on at age two and Michelle at age 42. "Michelle has been very active in my life since her passing. She gives me unbelievable signs. So does Holly, but Michelle seems to be in the forefront doing incredible things. I feel Michelle sleep with me at night. I have felt her presence sitting on the bed to the point where I put my hand on the bed to make sure I wasn't imagining it."

Mary B reports, "I actually heard Chaz's voice. I had my routine down: after work, as soon as I hit the doors to the parking lot, the tears would start. It was about a 40-minute drive home. After the tears were over I was driving and thinking about my latest work problems when I heard his voice. He shouted at me, like he was shouting across a football field or something. He said 'Mom, Mom, you have days that absolutely suck.' I just about drove off the road and yet several days later I was trying to talk myself out of it. I wanted to hear from him so badly that I thought I must have imagined it. I finally realized that wasn't true and there were ways to talk to him."

Zenzi's mom **Annie** explains that our children's voices can be recorded through noise or sound. "I'd turn the shower on, ask a question, and then leave a pause. Then I'd ask another question, pause, and then go back and listen to the recording. I have one recording that I heard. "Aim equal." Leukemia spelled backwards was a message to me one night in what I will call a dream visit. I asked why and I heard, 'Spell leukemia backwards' so I did and it sounds like *aim equal*. Zenzi was all about equality and loved to spell things backwards and say words backwards. So that was really mind boggling six months after they transitioned."

Kelley says that her daughter Aleia is "a strong, strong communicator. I heard her voice the day after she transitioned. Even in my saddest moments, she'd make herself known. She'd make herself clear."

Patty M, Adam's mom, says: "The day Adam passed, I saw him sitting on my feet. He was physical, I saw him with my eyes. He was shimmering but a little bit opaque. There was just a little bit of a difference. Then two years later on Mother's Day, I saw him in the most beautiful visit that completely changed my life and beliefs. He smiled at me and the look he gave me! My heart was charged with thousands of volts of energy. He nodded his head like, "It's me, Mom!" He was radiant and he had his cool white cap and his white hoodie and he just looked like the 17-year-old happy Adam that I always have known."

Lisa W has two boys in spirit: Michael passed on at age 12 and Anthony at age 18. "I'm a medium; shortly after I clairvoyantly saw my mother, I started seeing all kinds of children everywhere. It was the other children who convinced me that my own children were with me because I could validate evidence of what I was seeing with others. However, with my own children it was more difficult for me to feel and to understand. I had to manage that delicate dance between grief and awakening — where we know and understand that it's simply a new way of being with our kids — a new relationship."

"Early on I did see Andrew," explains his mom **Christine M.** It was shortly after his burial that I was awakened in the middle of the night for some water and had gone down the stairs. I didn't have my glasses on so I couldn't see a thing really but I saw just a blurry image on the couch. I felt guided to walk right up to him. I felt that I was able to see but not touch or say anything to him – but he was there. When I looked into his face, there was no fear; I knew it was him but his face was energy. I felt his energy and I walked to the water cooler in the kitchen. As I took a drink of water I watched him out of the side of my eye. Then I felt guided back upstairs. It was almost like an out-of-body experience." Andrew was 18 when he crossed to the other side.

Anna had been meditating for 15 years when Alexander passed. "So I immediately turned to meditation. Then, a couple of days after his passing, he came to me in the most remarkable way. I was sitting there, and he just showed up. He was so beautiful, even more than when he was on earth, with his blonde hair and big smile. He had this wonderful light and wonderful peace around him. He said,

'Mom, I'm doing okay.' That was the first sign he's not gone. His body is gone, but Alexander is still right here supporting us."

Telepathic Communication

"I had words popping into my head... simple as that. A very wise friend suggested I write those words down and they became phrases, then sentences, then paragraphs and pages."

— Joanna, Peter's mom

Telepathy is the communication of thoughts or ideas by means other than the known senses. It's kind of like having a conversation in your head with your loved one. Many parents tell us about their ability to hear from their children in this manner. Similarly, some also hear from their children through automatic writing. Also known as intuitive writing, this is a method of sitting quietly with pen in hand, asking questions, and writing down whatever is received. The goal is to allow the messages to flow. Most parents say when they look later at what they wrote, it absolutely sounds like their children.

Chandra's son Naman was 17 when he changed worlds. "Very early on after he passed, I realized that I was receiving signs. Now that I'm further down the path, I am able to hear him in my head. As a clinical psychologist, I know there is already a lot of science about this and it will take time to be in our textbooks. This is something that cannot be explained and for me it's just a natural process. There is a lot about spirituality and the way we sense our children that is very different so I ask parents to be kind to themselves and not self-diagnose 'Am I crazy?'"

Tyler, **Pat**'s son, was 20 when he made his transition to spirit. "I felt him with me as I searched for ways to channel my grief. I could feel him pushing me into certain places that I never would have gone. He was always there behind me, saying, 'I can help you from the other side, Mom. I can help you.' And he did. He always has."

Alessandro was 20 when he moved into another realm. His mom **Ana E** had a question for her son: "After he passed I would step outside my house and sit on the steps. I asked him, 'Did you do it? I mean, did you jump?' I had that uncertainty. I didn't know if he had purposely jumped or if it was an accident. And I kept hearing, 'It was an accident, Mom, it was an accident.'"

Lisa A interacts with her son Derry through a game. "Oh, it's so fun! From day one we started playing what we call 'theme of the day'. We have a chalkboard in our home and whatever word pops into my head during meditation, I write it down and see where it will show up. It can be something that has recently happened, because there's no sequential time from my son's point of view. Or it could be something that might happen in the near future." Derry was 20 when he passed on.

Chris V also plays a game with her son. "Daniel and I play Wordle together every single day. I just listen and he gives me the letters. We always figure out the puzzle together."

Joanna is mom to Peter who crossed over at age 22. "My communication with Peter started in the hospital around the time he was crossing over. I had words popping into my head, simple as that. A very wise friend suggested I write those words down and they became phrases, then sentences, then paragraphs and pages. This was over a period of months. Though I'm hopeless with meditation, I can click into a meditative state in order to receive words very easily. They started off as chats from Peter, very much in his vocabulary and then they developed over time into what I describe as mind-blowing missives of great wisdom in a variety of styles. I feel privileged to be able to access what I think is the bigger picture."

"I learned intuitive writing through Helping Parents Heal," explains Mia's mom, **Ramona.** "I didn't know if anything would happen. I meditated to the best of my abilities on the first day and said, 'Okay, I'm going to see what happens.' I wrote about five pages without putting my pen down: there were messages addressed to me and others. Messages about our souls – very deep stuff that I was just beginning to become aware of. So I'm pretty sure it didn't come from me. English is not my first language and there were words that I don't use in my vocabulary."

Babette has found that her son Daniel has taught her a lot. "After Daniel transitioned, he talked to me but I assumed it was just my thoughts. But then he told me things that proved it really was him. I started writing everything down and have all these journals with messages from him. It's just amazing. Messages such as 'love is all there is' and 'love is the only thing that's real'. He told me he could be in many places at the same time and I'd never heard of that. He's been an amazing teacher."

Carolyn C's 16-year-old daughter Cara passed on unexpectedly. "Taking courses really helped me silence the mind by sitting in silence as a daily practice. Eventually, I learned how to spirit-write, where Cara's putting the thoughts in my head that I'm writing down. It took a lot of patience and time and practice."

Mabel's ongoing communication with her son Leo, who changed worlds at age 19, brings comfort to other parents as well. "Leo's communication comes so naturally. I don't even have to ask. Sometimes it's his responses to my questions, and sometimes it's him helping me out of predicaments. His messages are always very helpful and healing. He made it very clear that he wanted to share this with other parents. So I keep writing and sharing on the HPH site. I'm very grateful when other parents find his messages comforting, inspiring, and uplifting."

Messages and Connections Through Other People

"I have frequently answered the phone and called out, 'Hey Lynn, I've got somebody on the line who says she has a message from Devon. He said he's not going to leave her alone until she relays it to you.' We just sit back and let it happen."

— Jeff H, Devon's dad

Sometimes our children communicate with us through other people. Parents will seek out a gifted medium who can make that connection with their child by providing evidential validations as well as messages. But other times, the messages are given to parents through a family member, friend, or even a stranger.

Colleen, whose son is Denis, says: "My sisters and I went to see a medium at a dinner. She came straight to the table and said to me: 'I have a very tall young man and he wants you to know that he can breathe. He can take a full breath, but he doesn't want to talk in front of everybody. He doesn't want all these people knowing his business.' It was my son."

"It sounds weird, but through Harry's transition, we've become closer than ever," says **Anne-marie** whose son Harry passed on. "I saw my first medium within three days. I had a mixed-up understanding; it was ignorance really because I was worried that Harry would get out of reach. We need to learn to trust our intuition and ability to hear them, although not necessarily with our ears. At that session, the medium said one especially interesting thing. Most of it was correct, but this one thing really stood out. Harry loved collecting, buying, working on, and selling cars; some of the parts were at my house. The medium said, 'Harry said he's sorry for the oil stains on your pavers'. It wasn't until I had cleared away this massive pile of car parts that I saw a huge oil stain which is permanently embedded in my brick pavers. I love that stain, and every time I see it, I think of Harry."

Lin's son Ryan changed worlds at age 26. "I often have other people tell me they had a dream about Ryan and have a message for me. Recently, I was looking through some photographs and came across Ryan's high school yearbook when he was dating a girl called Tasia. They had gone their separate ways and I hadn't heard from her in five years. I went to bed crying and wishing I could hear from her. The very next morning there was a text from Tasia that said: 'I had a dream about you last night. Are you okay?' That blew me away. The timing could not be a coincidence. So I met with her and asked her about her dream and she said: 'I hear from Ryan, I see Ryan, and dream about him, but last night was the first night he told me *I need you to do something for me. My mom needs you.*' So that's kind of the way he communicates with me. I don't see or hear Ryan, but I feel like I receive downloads."

Dolores's son Eric, who made his transition to spirit at age 24, was able to send her the hug she had been asking for. "In the beginning, I didn't have a clue about signs. I was crying daily and talking to Eric. I knew he was around and that he could hear me, but I couldn't hear him back. I was telling him how much I needed a hug. Around day ten, I went to a market. There were young people at tables taking donations for a very worthy cause that I recognized. I thought I'd donate and approached a young man who was the same age, height, build, and coloring of my son Eric. I talked with him as I was making my donation and he was very friendly – just like Eric. After he handed me a receipt, he said: 'How about a hug?' This took me by surprise. I mean, who does that? No one has ever asked me for a hug at one of those tables, not before or since Eric's passing. I had been asking for a hug and this was his way of giving me one. So I hugged this young man, and it felt like I was hugging my son. I walked away thinking, 'What just happened?' That was Eric."

Chelsea was two days old when she passed from this earth, and 23 years later her brother Morgan joined her at age 29. Their mom **Elizabeth** says, "Chelsea was the first person to meet Morgan when he transitioned at the base camp of Mount Everest. They have both shown me that it's possible to have communication with our kids. One of the things I have noticed is that they are very powerful, especially in the very beginning. I think it's probably because they really want to get the message through. During a reading with a medium, Morgan said to 'look up' and I wondered what that meant. The next day, a trapdoor on the garage ceiling was slid all the way open and underneath was an electric golf cart. We couldn't find the keys but moved it out of the way and closed the trapdoor. We thought it was the strangest thing; how could that have happened? The next day, the same thing happened again. I looked up and remembered what the medium had said. It was just like Morgan to do these crazy things."

Lisa's son Shayne passed on in her husband's arms. "For my husband, whose little girl passed on via cancer at the age of three, Shayne was the second child to die in his arms. I have a lot of gratitude that Shayne made us part of his transition and we could be there for him. I ended up speaking to a medium the next morning and the first thing she said was that Shayne was holding the hand of a little girl about three years old with red hair. My husband's little girl."

Wendy, whose Hugh passed on at age 20, says: "I hear other parents talk about seeing the signs right away after their children passed, but I did not. I'm pretty sure it's because I'm a very analytical and research-based person... very much in my head. I'm so grateful that Hugh found a way to get through to me through another person. He was always an excellent communicator and still is. About a week and a half after he passed, I got a text from a colleague who I didn't know very well. She said, 'You probably don't know this about me, but I've had some special psychic gifts since I was born. When I heard that your son had passed on, I was flooded with images and messages that I feel compelled to tell you if you're willing to listen.' I thought, 'Hot dang, you bet!' She told me some things that sounded exactly like what he would say. I left that conversation thinking, 'Wow! What just happened?'"

Other Creative Ways!

"We sense her presence because she's all around us. She moves things in our home; for example, our living room pillows end up in the kitchen."

— Michelle T, Jordan's mom

There are more ways that parents have heard from their children than we can count. Their kids move objects, use number sequences on license plates, send feathers and hearts, and even speak through a candle flame. There's no limit to what our kids will do to get our attention! Here are a few more amazing connections...

Jeff H, Devon's dad, describes his son's display of energy: "Devon is not subtle so it really hasn't been difficult to sense him. He has the ability to move objects and he almost always does it when there's someone else around so we have some independent confirmation. It usually happens when we're talking about him. He's knocked boxes off tables. He's even made rocks pop out of a flower pot."

Devon's mom, **Lynn**, says more about these telekinetic signs. "At Christmas once, in front of many other people, we were walking by a table full of candy and this box of candy literally leapt off the table. I kind of laughed and said, 'Oh Devon!' Another time we were in Boston with parents of one of Devon's friends. We were talking about Devon and a rock leaped out of a plant pot and they witnessed it also."

Margaret's son Kenny, who was 23 when he changed worlds, has moved some things in order to help his mom out. "I had a session with the medium Sue Frederick last year and we looked at what my and his purposes were together. It changed the whole way I looked at things. It turns out Kenny and I are partners and I have a mission. He helps me every day, not just with signs, but with other things. For example, I forgot my sunglasses and returned to the house to find them: there was my inhaler next to the glasses. I have bad asthma and didn't realize I had left the inhaler at home. He does things like that all the time."

Mike says, "One way Dylan connects with me is through numbers; I'll glance at a clock and it's 11:11. I'll get in the car and it's 1:11. It happens over and over and over, and I just tell him, 'Hope you're doing okay. Thanks for the sign.'"

Emma crossed over at age 15; her mom **Claudia** always thanks her daughter for the signs she sends. "About six months before Emma passed on, she started getting hearts. When she drank a glass of water and spilled some on her shirt, it was in a heart shape. When she walked on a pathway, she found a heart shape or puddle in a heart shape. I told her that I believed they were signs from God. The first signs I got from her after she passed on were hearts. I also found repetitions. For example, every day when I'm driving I see license plates with the numbers 0 4 7, which is the date she passed. I always say 'Thank you, Emma, I know you are with me'. When I acknowledge, I receive more. If I'm not sure, I ask for another one and get a repetition of it."

Tom shares: "I asked Kevin for guidance about 'Should I hire this person or not?' I had a 2 o'clock call with the candidate to see if we were going to move forward. Three minutes before 2pm, a car passed me and its license plate said '570 YES'. Five and seven were Kevin's varsity football numbers, and it happened at three minutes before 2pm which is 1:57."

"One of my favorite signs was on my birthday, the first one after Michele crossed over," says **Pamela**. "The backstory is that on her last birthday here, her friends threw her a party. They got a big poster and folded it in half into a birthday card that they all signed. Fast forward a year on my birthday. I don't really think much of birthdays, so I went up to her room to feed her cat. As I'm putting cat food on the floor, I hear a noise in her closet and I see something sticking out. I open the door and there's that giant birthday card!"

Josh's dad, **Andy**, shares: "He loves to give me feathers, coins, and little Nerf darts. I was raised as a fundamentalist Christian and they don't talk about things like that. After I came to HPH, I was kind of embarrassed when I first brought up his signs. It was like 'Is this a thing? Is this real?' I found out in the past four years that these signs are just as real, or even more so, than earthly reality."

Angela B tells us: "We went to a harbor after her service and found this heart with a small orange H and a blue circle. The message on it was 'keep on.' The bracelet she wore, which I'm wearing now, also says 'keep on.'"

"I've always 'felt' the other side," says Garrett's mom, **Laurie.** "I blocked it out for a long time. I was busy with kids and had a career. When my dad passed on, I could see him in our home. When my mom passed, I could see her. The night before my son transitioned, I saw my mom in my dining room, and I said, 'I hope you're not here for what I think you're here for.' So my soul kind of knew. Garrett ironically found a medium – a total stranger – who contacted me. Through her, I received messages about things she could not have known. So through his passing, and the other experiences I've had, I know our loved ones are simply in another world."

Lynn H feels that the signs from Devon fall right in line with his personality. "Devon knew how to get attention in this life and he knows how to get attention in the next life. He's in our face a lot. He knew how to get us to meet mediums. In the beginning, he switched lights on and off. When we talked about him, music turned on and off. Numbers have always been a big thing. We've actually seen him move things, with witnesses. In the beginning, even though I was a grieving mom, I couldn't wait to wake up just to see what was going to happen that day. But it wasn't all fun and games; there was a lot of sadness AND it was also an adventure."

Harry, **Anne-marie**'s son, found a unique way to connect with his mom. "Another thing that's happened to me twice is Harry speaking through a candle flame dancing in response to something I said. I have that on video. There was no wind in the room, and there was another candle right next to it that was steady. I can't make that happen at will. Maybe that took a huge amount of effort and he can't do it very often."

Kate's son Warren, who transitioned to spirit at age 17, wants to make sure his mom is in the spotlight. "He appeared in the light early on. Whenever I talked about my purpose, a light – like a spotlight – shined on me,. Other people can see this light as well. I sat between two friends on the day of his celebration of life and talked about knowing my purpose of pursuing advocacy and sharing my story about Warren. Suddenly there was this spotlight on me that my friends first noticed. This has happened several times."

Sensing Signs and Visits

"After Alexander transitioned, I felt he was communicating: 'I'm trying to find you and it's not easy. You need to raise your vibration. You need to become a brighter light.' When you expand your energy field through the process of raising your vibration, it ultimately allows you to see things from a higher perspective."

— Craig, Alexander's dad

Some parents wonder 'Why don't I get any signs?' Others aren't sure whether they are receiving signs and ask how to get them. Signs range from big, bold, and hard to miss to more subtle. Some evidence suggests that our kids often send signs; it's up to us to notice and be open to them. In their interviews, many Shining Light Parents shared wonderful suggestions on how to better sense signs and visits.

"It started with meditation," explains **Jayme** whose son Devon changed worlds at age 24. "I didn't really think you could connect to the other side through meditation until after my son passed. Once you can quiet your mind, you recognize the energy. When I feel his energy, I get emotional because he brings the love. Your children want you to know how much they love you and that they are there for you."

Mary D also finds meditation helpful to connect with her daughter Lea. "I feel like meditation has helped me. I can feel Lea's presence come closer. I feel into my auras or into my space when I'm in a deep meditation. Also, I'm also very aware of the subtle nudges to look down to see a heart-shaped rock, or to look up at an owl staring at me. Be mindful of those very subtle nudges because that's how simple it can be."

Carol K, mom to Kevin, says: "It's my openness that I believed right away, that this is really something. Your openness to it makes it easier for you to detect their presence."

Marie, Sienna's mom, explains: "In the early times it can be very hard, because our energy can be so dense and there are so many emotions about their passing. For this reason, it is sometimes hard to connect. But over time, finding the quiet moments and being able to be still in life really helps."

"I need to learn to quiet my mind", says **Beth**. "I know that I need to be accepting because I move too fast through the world. I need to stop and just see and feel more. I know our kids are still right here."

Paige's baby daughter, Jaimie, was stillborn. Years later after two miscarriages, her son Brian passed on at age 23. Paige says: "Energy work and meditation have been huge for me. I always recommend to parents and clients to consider learning some Reiki. Understanding that we're all energy and how that works is huge. My Reiki journey began before my contact with HPH; I believe it has contributed to how I sense Brian now."

Nancy, mother of sons Will and Joey, states: "I would say that interpreting connections with our children is like learning a new language or several languages. If you're open to it and give some reinforcement, it tends to stabilize over time. Lights, music lyrics, song titles, letters and numbers on license plates. Sometimes I can sense them kind of tapping a foot and waiting for me to get it, and then I get more. That's how it works."

Aiden, 15, and Conor 20, sons of **Kathy and Andy**, crossed over within 8 months of each other. Kathy advises, "Know yourself, know where your strengths are. Mine is clairsentience ('clear feeling' beyond what the five senses usually perceive). You can expand other ways to communicate through meditation and quiet the mind. I am not a great meditator so for me in the very beginning it was through running. I would get downloads of information. So know where you feel the most comfortable. Don't sit down in a quiet room and say 'Be quiet, be quiet, be quiet' if that's not your go-to. You can eventually learn."

Allison says that when she meditates with her son Davey, her body calms down. "I feel his love. It's beautiful. Another helpful way to connect is through acts of kindness. Instead of flowers or food, I asked people to do acts of kindness in Davey's name and share the stories. It helped me so much and made me feel his spirit living on through the stories. I wish I could share them all! Even today, I feel like Davey is sending me to do certain acts of kindness, and the two of us are high-fiving each other right after."

Maggie S, whose son Mitch crossed over at age 27, says: "In order to feel your child's presence, you have to heal the pain first. Then you'll be able to sense and start seeing the signs, believing, and looking at life from a different perspective."

"I use crystals and meditate a lot," says **Heather S** whose son Luke moved into the next phase of life at age 20. "There are some wonderful guided meditations to help parents. I've had excellent connections and visits with Luke. The first time, I did Reiki through a guided meditation and said: 'Luke, I really want to speak to you one on one, like you do with me through the mediums.' I did my chakras, grounding, and meditated, but I got nothing. That night as I was taking a bath, I was reading and I heard a voice in my head say, 'Meditate'. I thought 'I already meditated today, and I'm really enjoying this book.' Again, I heard: 'Meditate.' As soon as I closed my eyes and relaxed, Luke came in, it was his voice. We had a conversation and a connection, and he brought in one of my guides who said she was facilitating. She called herself an ancillary. I had a 20-minute visit with my son. I got out of the tub, got my pajamas on, and they were still talking and having a conversation with me. I said, 'Okay, guys, I hope we can do this again.' My guide said, 'Oh, you'll see, you will.' Luke said, 'Mom, I'm just a thought away, a thought away.'"

Linda O describes how she spends time with her son David. "I set up a sacred space with David's pictures and different things that were his. I'll sit for half an hour and put a couple of his favorite music tracks on and just spend that special time with him. That's helped to build communication."

Heather H's son Xavier Alexander graduated from earth-school at five months of age. "I've found that holding space and being quiet is key. I'm a chatterbox, internally too. It gets so busy inside but I'll stop and sit. It's uncomfortable but, usually after a few minutes, I start settling. My heart opens, and I can receive the message. I'll see little things, like colors, or angel numbers. During a psychic reading I was told my son loves the color yellow. When I become open I'll start seeing yellow. Often, I'm not even looking for it. If I doubt it, there will be more yellow until I notice. Then I pause and pay attention."

Sherry also found peace through meditation after the miscarriage of her baby Gabriel. "For me it is definitely meditation. I've had a practice now for over 15 years. Meditation has taught me to have heightened inner senses and really be aware that they exist. It's a layering effect. While sitting in silence, we're sometimes gifted with that vastness that you enter and feel suspended in. Sometimes there's spontaneous connection in that space and sometimes it's after meditation while you're taking a hike. That space can spill over into the day."

Cindy says, "I am a visual person and Josh was a visual arts person. Josh and I play this little game that he started early, where I'll say, 'Tell me something about your dad.' And he'll show me something, and I'll text my ex-husband and say, 'Tell me about this.' If you're a numbers person, an analytical type, and that's how you perceive the world, then focus on numbers, on mathematical things, focus on shapes. If you're a more visually creative-colors person, focus on smells and things of that nature. Think about who you are, about who your child is, and look for those things. And when you see them, never fail to say, 'I see you.' Once I started saying that, I could feel that joy come in immediately. It becomes a joyful game, but it doesn't happen overnight. It's a learning process."

Chris V says about her son Daniel, "I dedicate an hour of meditation a day to Daniel and most of the time I can hear him, although it's more like a 'knowing' and I can sense him."

When eleven-year-old Grant changed worlds, his mom **Carre** found a way to continue the relationship with him. "There's something called 'sitting in the spirit' to raise your vibration to connect. He started coming to my head. We have dance parties together because the way I raise my spirit is listening to music. I have a hard time meditating. I feel him come in first, and then I get my loved ones around, like in a circle. It's just like a big dance party to raise my vibration. That's always really fun."

69

Andrea's daughter Chloe communicates with her mom quite often. "I asked Chloe what she would like me to say in response to a question. She said, 'It's really *spirit time* that manages things.' So if you feel that contact isn't happening fast enough, or you haven't heard from your child, or you can't meditate, just sit still. Remember that things happen according to 'spirit time' and be patient with yourself. That's one of the big things that I learned. Another thing I learned is to cultivate a new relationship with your child. I have a bench that I go to and I'll say, 'Chloe I'm going at 10 A.M.' Some of the most amazing things have happened when I set a certain time to meet with her. They are busy too so it's nice to make an appointment."

Candi offers the wisdom that healing is important. "After James transitioned to spirit, I realized I was going to have to heal myself from the inside out before I could help others. Reiki helped a lot; so did being quiet and keeping my mind open. When your kids send you signs, realize that it is a little miracle and take time to really say thank you."

Davey's mom **Allison** shares, "My mantra was 'I want to feel you spiritually so I don't miss you so badly physically.' I focused on that every day. I had to raise my vibration by getting healthy, walking, eating right, etc. Then I'd get quiet and listen. I had to fake it sometimes by picturing him sitting next to me and I'd start talking. After a while, I'd get into it and was really talking to him."

Craig's son Alexander, who passed on at 16, helped his father know how to connect. "After Alexander transitioned, I felt he was communicating to me: 'I'm trying to find you and it's not easy. You need to raise your vibration. You need to become a brighter light.' He led me to teachings about chakras – energy centers through the body. This led me to doing Kundalini yoga for over six years now. It really helped me raise my vibration. When you expand your energy field, it eventually allows you to see things from a higher perspective. Our children are no longer encased in a physical body; they're out there in the universal field of energy. They can truly feel us more than ever because they're not enclosed. The more we enclose ourselves, the more we put ourselves in this box, the lower our vibrations become."

Trust and Believe

"The interesting thing is that it wasn't about Davey reaching out. It was about me allowing him in. That was the revelation – learning to get out of my own way."

— David A, father of Davey

Many parents ask, "How do I know it's really my child?" The only person who can answer that for certain is the parent. They know the instant recognition, understand the deep significance of the sign, and feel the profound resonance in their heart. When that knowing speaks, listen. It is your child. Trust and believe.

Parents often question themselves about whether or not the sign is real. **Ana M** has no doubt that her sons Franky and JoseLuis are around. "We feel them. There is a feeling that is also called intuition. Don't disregard it. Is it there? Your first answer is the answer. Don't doubt it."

Carolyn trusts the signs that her daughter Cara brings in. "First is really believing and trusting. I would get physical sensations and I just couldn't wrap my head around it, but I learned how to trust."

Christiane, whose son David passed on at age 18, says: "I have found journaling is really helpful for me to connect with David. I also enjoy the animal of the week that the medium Christine Salter posts on Facebook for parents. When I do get one of those signs, it's a moment where I feel joy and connection. I know he's here with me. I think you really have to have that mindset. It is only a thin veil that separates us from the way that we would like to be together."

Truc-Co's daughter Ailee transitioned to spirit at age 2. "I've had to learn to trust myself. Sometimes that voice in my head is telling me one thing, and my heart is feeling something else. Each of us is different in how we receive signs. At first, when my husband received signs, I internally asked myself: Why didn't I get it?' or 'Why can't I receive it the way he did?' I'm learning to put that aside and trust myself. I believe that the way I receive my signs is the way it's supposed to be. It's not a competition."

Ailee's father **Tom J** agrees with his wife Truc-Co. "We've learned that there is no one-size-fits-all. Signs like pennies or feathers are just one way of communicating. I would say not to get too fixated on 'This person asked for a sign and got it. How come I'm not getting it?' That sign may not be relevant to you. These days, we're getting so many signs that we don't even call them signs anymore. It's just regular everyday communication. We interact with her every day like we used to, but in a slightly different format."

Marc, Zenzi's father, tells us: "It's getting out of my own way and asking. I did not have a consistent meditation practice until Zenzi transitioned. It's just trusting and remembering. Anytime I ask, Zenzi shows up right away even though I know they're busy doing other things."

Danny relates: "I've learned to trust the signs and messages. Initially, you wonder if you're going crazy. The signs may not always be from Ethan, but I try to understand what the universe is trying to convey to me."

For **Jean,** whose son Joseph passed on, trust is the key. "I learned that spirit is very patient with my doubts. Many times, I've thought, 'Oh, is that just a coincidence?' To be sure, I'll ask for something more specific and – without a doubt – every time I get it."

Reese's mom **Rhonda** says, "I call it 'Knowing' with a capital K. You just *know*. It took a while to sink in, to really believe the whole spirit thing. Some people aren't open to this, but I chose to believe."

Sandra had already received signs from her mother who passed on before her 30 year-old son Josh transitioned from earth. By journaling and taking pictures of the signs, she was able to go back and be amazed at Josh's communication with her. She beautifully explains how her connection with her son continues: "I had a pretty open mind about it. My mother crossed over many years ago when I was pregnant with Josh. I felt like I got signs from her over the years, but thought 'Maybe my head is playing tricks on me?' Immediately after Josh passed on, he started being present, loud and clear. At first, the signs really weren't pleasant. For example, the homicide detective had just left the house, and I went to get some Advil out of the cabinet. When I opened it, everything came down – all the shelves. *Boom*!"

Sandra continues, "I questioned myself whether I wanted to hear from him so much that I imagined these things. I was hesitant about who to share them with. The very first time I went to see a medium, the signs were confirmed. I'm talking about unusual things – not common ones like a feather or bird. Then I started journaling about them and taking pictures. Signs started happening with other people around to witness them. I now know for a fact that death is not the end. If I thought death is the end, I don't know that I would have healed the way I have... that my journey would be where it is today. My relationship with Josh has continued to grow. I know that might sound strange, but it really has. We've had so much more time together, more than we had near the end of his life here."

Chapter 3: Finding Meaning and Purpose

by Allison Alison

A particularly challenging question for Shining Light Parents is about there being a meaning and timing behind their child's passing. As parents grappled with responses, they seemed to discover new insights. Many parents concluded that their child's passing did involve a greater meaning and timing. While a few parents felt lingering anger, most came to terms with their child's passing and discovered new meaning behind it.

Some parents found a purpose that allowed them to give back in a positive way. Others, upon reflecting on the days or months preceding their child's transition, noticed signs that suggested their child knew what lay ahead.

Through an exploration of the afterlife and reconstructing their child's final moments on earth, some parents concluded that *soul plans* may have existed between them and their child. While the parent's human brains and hearts may struggle to accept this, their inner heart and awareness recognized it as true. For newly grieving parents, the notion that they could have *willingly chosen* such a horrible experience may seem unfathomable. Angry parents have asked, 'Why would I ever elect to endure such excruciating pain?' Why, indeed, would anyone opt for this? Yet, as they searched for understanding and learned more about the afterlife, the possibility of *pre-birth planning* resonated with some parents.

When searching for meaning behind their children's transition from earth, some parents explored the idea of *exit points*. This is the theory that souls choose possible times when they will leave their physical bodies and return to the afterlife. Some parents looked at their children's lives and realized there were previous times when they could have passed on but did not. Parents considered the possibility that their children exited at this time for higher purposes: for their soul growth and / or for the soul growth of others.

After reflecting, some parents felt that their children were *advanced souls* who accomplished all they had come to do in this lifetime. (Another term for this is 'old soul'. However, clinical evidence suggests that the level of energy / soul evolvement is more due to learning and growing versus how long the soul has existed.)

Parents hope that they will transition from earth before their children. When that doesn't happen, self-realization, meaning, and service to others can help parents find the strength to live on and connect with their children.

Purpose

"I am developing an entirely new belief system as a direct result of my son's passing. This helps me evolve as a human and a parent. I found that accepting new spiritual concepts lessened the pain of missing his physical departure. It opened up a pathway of peace that I didn't know was even possible. I learned that his early exit was designed to help us become who we are truly meant to be in this life. My willingness to find space in the moment — to quiet my mind intentionally and just be – is new for me but this is where I find him."

— Galen, Weston's mom

Parents discovered profound meaning after their child's passing that led them to embrace newfound purposes. For some, this journey led to greater spiritual awakening. Others found themselves empowered to make positive changes in the world in their child's honor. Some parents provided support to other grieving parents by offering solace and guidance.

Others endeavored to spread love, kindness, and help illuminate the world.

Craig, along with many others, exemplifies this spiritual growth after his son Alexander changed worlds. "I believe our children come here for a purpose. I don't think it's a fluke that we just magically appear. I think there's a purpose behind all this existence. I feel we are all here to grow into a higher state of grace and love. I believe our children have this experience with us because they're trying to help us evolve into higher beings."

Wendy explains her son Hugh's crossing over as a trigger event: "It created this amazing spiritual opening for me, an awakening. My passion now is working with Helping Parents Heal by co-leading a group to support other parents on this journey. It's my life's work now."

Jayme also felt spiritual growth for her family and explains, "I had to convince my husband to have a fourth child because I was always concerned one of them would pass on. I kept them close, we did a lot together, and have all those memories. My oldest went through a rough patch with a drug addiction but he recovered. When Devon passed on, I realized he was the one I was worried about. However, I feel he left for the growth of my soul and our family's souls. I do feel like he left for us."

Ramona feels that she is growing spiritually and says: "I can look at things two different ways. One is that the universe is total chaos, and everything happens randomly. Some people are lucky; they get to keep all their kids, and some people are not that lucky. That is a terrible way of looking at things. I choose to look at things in ways that make me feel alive. Maybe there is a soul plan but I don't think everything is set in detail. I think there is an outline, but we still have free will. About purpose – I have thought about this for almost four years since Mia passed on. I want to do something good, to help the person next to me. I like to believe that I'm growing spiritually because of this experience. My purpose, I think, is to feel alive."

Some parents felt this purpose with the help of spirit guides. **Janean** explains, "There was a specific time, about two years before Sean passed, that I was adoring him. I was watching the kids out the window. We had just come back from vacation, and they were supposed to be cleaning our boat. Sean was snapping towels at his sister, and they were goofing around. I was just staring at him, so in love and feeling so lucky. There was a voice in my head – I had never experienced that before. It said things are not always going to be this way."

Janean continues, "At first, I passed it off as mother-paranoia. But when he was spiralling down, I was out for a run one day and praying while I ran. I prayed in the traditional way and asked God to work through Sean's experience and the trials he was going through. He was such a good person; I knew he could have turned it around and helped a lot of people. That same voice said, 'Your prayers are not going to be answered the way you want them to be.' That took me to my knees, and I was sobbing on the forest floor. After he passed on, I was out hiking and came across that same place. I got a sense that I was told ahead of time that it was out of my control and there was a greater purpose. That was incredibly comforting. At the time, I didn't know what that voice was, but now believe it was a spirit guide, angel, or some sort of messenger. I needed that because, with a child passing by suicide, there is a lot of guilt."

Carol reiterates this point: "When tragedy strikes, your angels, guides, Universe, your Higher Power... they all converge to help you counteract the tragedy by spreading more light and more peace in the world."

Louise and her daughter Jilly who is in spirit are writing a book together. "My daughter correctly predicted her bodily death and the manner. About a month before she passed, I was driving with her sitting next to me and I did a U-turn. She grabbed my arm and said, 'This is how it's going to happen Mom – the car accident I'm going to die in. It's going to happen on a turn. I'm going to get hit in the side.'"

Louise continues: "Jilly wrote us letters two days before she transitioned thanking us for being good parents. When the accident happened, she was a passenger, and her best friend was driving. Jilly was killed instantly at the age of 19. The morning she died, I woke up at 6am and didn't know why. This turned out to be the time of the accident. She drew the scene of the accident in art class when she was a junior in high school – two years before it happened. She showed the car being hit in the side, exactly as it really happened. In the corner of this picture were the Twin Towers with a plane going into them. I didn't understand that connection until I realized the last night she spent on earth was with friends who are twins. Their birthday is September 11th.

Louise concludes: "On our way to the accident scene, they called me and told me she was gone. I immediately heard her say in my mind, 'It's OK, Mom. I jumped and didn't feel a thing.' One of our mottos is, 'If life throws bricks at you, pick them up and build something with them.' So we are writing a book together."

Some parents find purpose in their child's illnesses and work to help others. **Tava** explains, "In a way, with Christina the timing and the way she transitioned actually helped. It may sound odd, but I now know that all had to happen for me to become awakened. There have been thousands and thousands of people that have been helped because of who she was and how she transitioned. I heard from people around the world about how they're now getting medical help for *dysautonomia* – different parts of the autonomic nervous system failing. If Christina hadn't transitioned the way she did, they may not have."

Beth corroborates this sentiment, "The meaning of Steven's physical death was for me to grow, raise awareness about pediatric cancer, and meet special people. Erin's death, I'm still trying to figure that one out."

With their child's help many parents found purpose in honoring their child's passions. **Marie** published a picture book with her daughter Sienna's poems. "Sienna changed worlds at a very heavy time in humanity. We were locked down in Australia for six or eight weeks prior to her passing, and just before she passed, she wrote this poem. *Small Things: Sometimes you can't see them, sometimes you treasure them, but they are always there, whether you see them or you don't. Like butterfly eyes and bees and everything in between, a nicely made bed and a kiss on your head.*

Marie continues: "I feel as if her passing was a reminder at a time when everybody around her was fearful about what the future was going to hold. They had her poem etched into the playground at her school to remind people that, in the turmoil and the hardness of life, it's just those small things that matter. But sometimes it's the things that you can't see: that's our kids and their energy. Her dream was to be an author, so I published a picture book called *'Travel the Mind'* that has her poem in it."

Sue shares how organ donation gave her meaning: "With Kyle being an organ donor, we heard from people who received his organs. I was very aware that our worst day was the best day for multiple people."

Many parents feel an overwhelming purpose to help others because of their child's transition to the afterlife. **Jean** shares this sentiment: "I think, on the soul level, Joseph knew and I knew, too. I feel like the reason was so I could help so many other people."

Kate, whose son Warren transitioned from earth, states, "I think we have a plan and work to do together, especially to help others. Young people need to know they have a purpose. I believe that's what really keeps us here, finding our meaning and purpose in life."

Chandra went back to school after her child Naman crossed over. "I never thought I would become a student at my age and earn a PhD. When I look back, it's all because of my child. He kind of pushed me into this, saying, 'If my passing by suicide put you in this position, then I think you should know more about it.' I am now researching how children can be helped."

Whether helping one person or many, these parents have found purpose in being a shining light to others. **Louis** shares, "We started sign language classes for our son Joe when he was a year and a half old. Another family joined us for the classes, and their son Brian and Joe became best friends. After Joe passed on, Brian and I have met once a week for 13 years to share in our grief and support each other. That taught Brian how to not be afraid of death when he was diagnosed with and recovered from cancer."

Deb shares, "This wakeup call that I received after Dean's transition has reminded me about why I'm here: to model love and allow others to be whoever they are."

Some parents have found purpose by forgiving those who caused their child's bodily death. **Conrado**, whose son Nicolas passed on in a terrorist attack states, "There was a foreshadowing that he told us about. The meaning for me has been to stop hate because he was taken out by hate. Somebody had hate in their heart, and they did something terrible to so many people. What really got to us to stop hating is that we received so much love from so many people – even strangers. Everybody was calling and supporting us. We have to stop hating, even if it's one person at a time."

Rick and his wife Beth share this compassionate message about the person who caused the passing of their two children. "I looked up the drunk driver, but we didn't put any energy into him. After 13 years in prison, he became a minister and has helped people in Iowa for six years. Beth started to think about soul contracts and the minister being part of it; not only with us, Jess, and Josh. He had to be part of it as well. We made the decision to go to Iowa, meet with him and, forgive him. If we let him know what we've done with our lives since then, it would enable him to help other people."

Some parents have found silver linings in their child's passing. **Mike** explains what he learned after Dylan's passing, "If you look for silver linings in the tragedy of 'losing' your kids, you can find things that are very positive."

Marla – mom of Shane, Nicole, and Ryan who are in spirit – states, "Never compare your journey with anyone else's. We each are different and our children are different. Our life paths are different. It's important to honor where you are and what's happening for you. We created a 'silver lining list' in the Tampa HPH group. Each of us talked about something positive that unexpectedly came in. Every single person was able to do that. For me, it was being able to step into the healing work that I'm doing and help other parents get through it. I'm helping people with losses of all kinds. That's very meaningful to me."

Knowing

"Everyone in our family – my wife, Josh's mom, and his brothers – all knew he was going to pass on. We didn't know how or when, there was just 'a knowing'. We quietly talked about it on occasion. He loved to be a director and loved filming; that was his big thing in high school. He created a storyboard about a kid who bought a car, who was speeding and hit a tree and passed. It had to happen specifically for his mom's awakening and my awakening. I've learned things that I had no clue existed. Now I know what is real."

— Andy, Josh's dad

After their child's transition, some parents realized they were warned and prepared beforehand. Upon reflection, they recognized sensing something significant before their child passed. In hindsight, they became aware of intuitive feelings or recalled their child's words. This realization brought with it an understanding that there is more to this existence than meets the eye. These forewarnings encouraged them to delve into the mysteries of the afterlife.

Irene recalls, "My daughter Carly Elizabeth came into this world screaming; she was full of life, vibrant, a great kid. She went to Boston College, was brilliant, loved school, and wanted to be a teacher. But I had a gnawing feeling and worried that Carly was not going to be here for a long time. Soon after, she was diagnosed with gastric cancer and passed on in 2013 – only four months after the diagnosis."

Lisa shares, "I had this immediate knowing that Derek's transition happened exactly how it was supposed to happen. It almost didn't matter how he left his body. He woke up before the rest of us. He moved from his body to re-emerge into all that we are."

Elizabeth always worried about Morgan, "I believe there was definitely a timing and a meaning. Before he left for China, he said, 'Mom I don't think I'm coming back from China this time.' I said, 'Morgan, you don't even have to go, you have enough university credits, there's no reason for you to go, just stay here, be a cheerleader and have fun'. He said, 'No Mom, I'll be okay.' I think he knew that he was going to transition early. From the time that I held him in my arms when I first had him, I knew I wasn't going to have him long. I was a 'helicopter' mom to Morgan – always hovering over him! I wanted to know where he was going, and wanted to make sure he was safe. With my two daughters, I never felt that way; I didn't understand why back then, but now I know."

Colleen states, "In the beginning after his passing, I thought: 'How could this happen?' But then, when I reflected on it, I've always known that Denis wasn't meant to be here for a long time. There was a nagging in my brain that said: 'Hold on to this, he's not going to be here long'."

Megan also had a premonition: "I never felt like Lane was going to be with me for very long, but I didn't want to sit with that feeling. I thought I was just paranoid, but then I remembered I had a dream when he was a baby. He and his sister, who were only two years apart, were in the bath together. In this dream, my spirit guide came to me and said: 'You can only save one of them'. I woke up from that dream feeling very upset. I asked other people, 'What was that?' and they said, 'Oh don't worry, it was just a dream'. But it felt very real to me."

Mary says, "When Katherine had her cardiac arrest and we started CPR, I realized that I knew this would happen all along – like I'd seen it before. That really shocked me. Katherine was at a place in her life where she had met a lot of her goals. She had a very difficult struggle with mental illness, but she was doing fantastic. I think it was just her time."

"I definitely do think there was a meaning" said **Lynn**. "I had thoughts while Devon was in college that he might pass young but, strangely, it never bothered me. It was just in the back of my mind."

Mary shares this about her son, "Chaz told me that he was never meant to live a long life. It could have been an accident, illness, or most anything but his window for passing on had arrived. He told me in spirit that he met the goals of several people, not just myself, by passing when he did. That's exactly the type of thing he would have said when he was here so I wouldn't feel guilty."

Lisa W relates, "My son told me three things that I could go back and relate to. When Anthony was two years old, he said, 'I waited forever to come and be your baby'. When he was four, he said 'When I'm 18, I'm going to leave you and I'm so sad.' I said, 'Baby, when you're 18 you're a big boy and you go to college. It'll be okay.' When he crossed over, he was 18. I reflected back that no four-year-old would think that. Where did he get that? Six months before Anthony passed, he was getting ready to go to college and he said, 'Mom, I need to talk to you. I'm afraid I'm going to die. I keep feeling like I'm going to die. I need you to watch out for me.' I can't argue against the view that our souls sometimes know. Many of us within this group had that knowing, that feeling – that's our soul's awareness."

Anna got a gift after her son Alexander changed worlds. "Nobody told us about this recording until about three months after his passing. One of his teachers gave it to us with all the other things from school. When we heard his voice and he was giving us all these life lessons, we were crying our eyes out but also smiling. It's like he knew he was going to pass, and he wanted to give us this gift of love and tell us to keep going: you're going to stay here for a while so take advantage of life."

Patty's son Adam showed his precognition when he was young through drawings. "When Adam was in grade one, he constantly did these funny things. He painted pictures with little headstones and put his name on them or he painted a picture of a car accident. He did these things that would make me scratch my head. I believe they were signs from the universe like 'This is a heads up'. I pushed a lot of them away but, now that I look back, they were there."

Through her actions, **Patricia**'s daughter conveyed her knowing. "I feel like Melissa didn't have to be here as long as other people. She already knew. She got it before I did, and she changed everyone in the family. She would walk into a room and, if there was tension – stupid family things going on – she would be like, 'Come on, people'. She knew how to light up a room. I feel that she was here for a reason: to wake us all up."

Amy received a message from her child Brandon that gave her great comfort, "We had this beautiful conversation on our last night, to say, 'I'm here to support you. Tell me what I can do for you. I love you and have a beautiful evening.' What a gift that was! That seemed to have come as a blessing and I don't know the source of that, but it showed up in my life."

Mabel holds on to a special message that her son relayed to her at a young age. "My son Leo is my only child. He was and still is incredible. He is vibrant and energetic, loved to learn, excelled at school, and at whatever he was interested in like playing music. He was kind and helpful. He was talented yet humble. He was and still is passionate about making this world a better place. Leo was also very generous and compassionate; he even reached out to help kids who had bullied him in the past. When he was eight years old, he said to me, 'You know our mother and son bond can never be broken.' I was speechless."

Annie's child left a special message that shows an inner knowing about imminent passing. Annie says, "We asked Zenzi to change the quote on the whiteboard in the kitchen because the other quote had been there forever. Then we forgot about it. When we came back to our home after the transition, we couldn't imagine moving forward in life. But there was Zenzi's updated quote: 'It is the unknown we fear when we look upon death and darkness, nothing more.'"

Pamela shares a story about her daughter **Michelle** that shows knowing and awareness can come from otherworldly assistance. "Between the ages of three and six, she told me that she saw spirits. At the time, I was pretty skeptical and just thought she was playing around. She eventually grew out of it or, at least, stopped telling me about it. But she came to me two days before she passed on and said, 'Mom, remember when I was little, and I was seeing spirits. I think I'm seeing them again.' They had come to take her home; spirits and ancestors do come and help us to cross over."

Sherry got help from her grandfather in spirit. She explains, "The pregnancy was not planned and was a surprise. I was 40 years old and getting our oldest child ready for college. However, a year before becoming pregnant, I woke up and right next to me stood my grandfather who had passed on. He appeared milky in color, but I could see his full form from the torso up. I could make out his face and his magnificent smile and I could see the joy. He stayed just long enough that I didn't doubt that I was awake. When I joined Helping Parents Heal, I thought, 'Oh my goodness, he popped in to let me know that life continues.' It was such a comfort."

Claudia found comfort in how her daughter moved into the afterlife. She says, "Emma was a happy and healthy child. As she grew up, she was very kind, but above all, she was a provincial gymnast. This was her passion; she had done gymnastics since she was three years old. At age 12, she was diagnosed with bone cancer and had her leg amputated. The cancer came back when she was 15. She knew that this was going to be the end. When she passed on, she looked up in the corner of the room and said in a very contented voice: 'Oh, my God, Mommy, it's time for me to go,' and that was it. This was a gift because I knew she was not lost, she was not gone, and she was not alone. She's still with me."

Soul Planning

"I truly believe in a soul plan. I've been to a medium who said Jordan's first exit point was at age 25 and he passed less than two weeks from his 26th birthday. I think this soul plan and this challenge was built in for me. It was something that I could expand and grow from. Being part of Helping Parents Heal is helping me so much as I help others. I feel like my life has transformed for the better. We can't go back so going forward is what I'm excited about."

— Barb, Jordan's mom

The concept of a pre-existing soul plan before entering this realm has gained significant traction in recent years. This idea has been examined and reaffirmed in Robert Schwartz's books. Dr. Pitstick discusses it in article #25 at SoulProof.com and created an audio program that is in the Resources chapter. The best clinical evidence for pre-birth planning comes from the work of Michael Newton PhD who founded Life Between Lives therapy.

Numerous parents turn to this notion when grappling with the seeming injustices and complexities of their child's transition from earth. By contemplating the possibility of soulful plans being involved, parents find more peace amidst the anguish. They recognize that their child's journey is part of a much greater, fair, and purposeful design. The notion of soul contracts is familiar to many HPH parents. Some embrace it while others are less convinced. The important thing is that we can talk about it and think it through.

Lisa expands on this view. "Early on after Shayne's transition, he came to me and told me to read *Journey of Souls* by Michael Newton. He specifically recommended certain chapters about life selection and choosing a body; this totally resonated with me and my husband. I also read Robert Schwartz's book which indicates we agreed to a life plan. I look at the work we are currently doing – helping other parents and giving them tools to connect with their kids – and know it's our purpose."

Babette, Daniel's mom, explains how a HPH online class presenter opened her up to this idea. "My grandmother and mother both had NDEs back when no one talked about it. So I grew up knowing their stories and that there was meaning behind that. Then I heard Sara Ruble speak about soul plans. Her clarity has helped me; it all just makes sense to me. It's a blessing because, if you know there's a plan, you know you couldn't have actually changed anything. Parents who have dealt with addiction and suicide really take on guilt and blame. If you believe there's a plan behind it, then you can let go of that."

Cathy says, "I absolutely believe in soul planning. I know for a fact that I'm a better person now than I was when Ross was here. I wasn't a terrible person, but now I have a more open heart and compassion for people. I live one day at a time with my son and try to be of service during the time that I'm here."

Cindy states, "I don't believe that everything in the universe is predestined, but I think that there are plans. I'm a big believer in soul planning: what that means to me personally is our time here on earth is potentially one of many. It's not a punishment to any of us to be here; it's an exploration. That's why I say, 'Just stay curious.' We're here to experience something and have self-growth. If you shift your thinking to, 'What if I chose this?' What if we all sat around this table with whatever greater beings you believe in and said: 'I really want to learn this'? Absolutely, there was a purpose to Josh's passing. I talk about getting straight through the grief as opposed to going around it. My running route is right past the tree where his accident happened so I continue to run that way. About two months after his passing, I was running by there and I stopped in my tracks. I felt Josh there. I knew at a soul level that everything is happening as it should. I came to accept that."

Davey's parents both had enlightening talks with him the day he transitioned. This led them to believe in soul plans. **Allison** states, "I talked to Davey the morning of his accident and he said, 'Mom I'm so excited to talk to you about this. I know God exists.' I said, 'Davey, this is so cool. I can't wait to talk, but you're freaking your dad out. Your dad's not sure what's going on here. Could you just tone it down a little?' And he said, 'Mom, you never have to worry about me. I'll never leave you. You just *get* me, you're my soulmate.' I had never heard that before. I feel like I got this gift. When he transitioned, I knew he wasn't gone. He's physically not here, but he's not *gone*."

Merle feels certain that some form of pre-birth planning occurs. "I definitely believe in soul planning. I knew from when Chris was a young child that I was not going to have him forever. Chris' early exit was predestined. I still don't like it. But, at the end of the day, I know that the minute I transition, my beautiful boy is going to be right there to meet me. If we can accept and understand that, there is some peace."

"I believe that everything is timed, that the soul journey is taking us exactly where we need to go each day," **Sara** shares. "This brings me so much peace of mind. I look back at that shock in 1994 and now realize that Scott was meant to go at that time. I'll just trust in the whole big picture that Scott and I planned. The more you're invested in this, the more you learn the depth of this. You begin to see that everything in your life is there to teach."

Carolyn couldn't believe that the way and timing of her daughter's passing was just senseless. "I couldn't accept that this was just a random accident. As I learn more, soul planning does resonate with me. Thinking back, Cara used to tell me all the time that she didn't want to grow up and I think that she knew. I think her soul knew that she wasn't going to be here long. She was such an amazing person – amazing to not only her family but all of her friends. She taught us so much. I think that now she can do even more good on the other side and reach more people. So, yes, I really do believe that she planned to leave early and that it was going to be the hardest lesson of our lives. It would break our hearts open, but we would find a way to learn about this and to understand this."

Claudia says, "I strongly believe there is a soul plan. At first, I thought that idea was insane. How could I possibly choose to come to earth and experience all this? I don't have words for what it was like going through cancer with my daughter Emma. How could we possibly choose that? But if I don't believe there was a plan, then it doesn't make any sense at all."

Carol also feels certain. "I one-hundred-percent believe in a soul plan and that we cannot change the outcome. I believe that when our kids finish what they came here to do, they have exit points. I know Tyler had an earlier exit point where he got really sick. At age 14, a virus went to his cerebellum and the doctors told us we were lucky because it could have been fatal. After, two different mediums said he had an exit point related to something with his brain at 14. I believe there's no guilt, regardless of how our children cross to the other side. I think it was their journey."

Bill V explains, "After my son Greg passed on, my initial response was it's the grace of God. But he has talked to me about that a lot. He said, 'It was your time to wake up, Dad'. Greg has confirmed to me in our conversations that it was part of our soul contract. We have traveled together over many lifetimes: he'd been my father, I'd been his father. This time it was his turn to be my son. We've learned over time to communicate with each other – to exchange love and light energy. That's why it comes so easily for me now because we've been practicing this for many, many incarnations. I believe Greg saved me. When he passed, it put me on my knees and I said to God 'Help me.' Otherwise, I would never have asked for help; I had a heart attack and didn't ask for help. I was always self-sufficient. But I went down on my knees, that's when miracles started to happen and Greg started to come through."

Heather could feel that she and her son had made a plan. "The girl who does my hair is a gifted psychic. She told me there was a lot of energy being directed towards earth, and a lot of souls were going to choose to exit. When she said that, something in my heart knew. I wasn't aware which one of my three children would pass, but I felt like something was coming. I feel like Luke and I made a plan together. This was going to happen, and it was going to completely open me up – which it has."

Kathy realized she could not control her children's lives and what happened to them. "I realized there is a bit of control I have over all of this. That control is in my choices now and the choice I made to come here and live this life. I always felt 'I'm the parent; I know everything. I should have controlled everything, I should have made their lives perfect'. Soul planning has helped me to embrace the fact that my children are each their own spirit. They came here with their own plans and we came here to do this together. I have learned along the way that they are my greatest teachers. I wasn't their greatest teacher; they have been mine and they continue to be. The plan continues – it didn't just stop after their transition. They're working there, my husband and I are working here, and we're building together."

The view that we each have a soul plan and purpose is reiterated by Mason's mom **Beverly**. "I believe that we have a plan and there's a greater masterpiece going on. In our human bodies, we're not able to see completely, maybe just a small piece of the plan. Our children's lives have a purpose, our lives have a purpose, and we're intertwined."

Mabel feels like she and her son made a soul plan. "I have no doubt that Leo and I agreed to a plan before this current life on earth. When I look back after all these years, the pieces fit together and the timing is divinely orchestrated. Leo was born on August 10 or 8-10 and his time of passing was exactly 8:10. There are no coincidences."

Marc adds, "What I signed up for, what Annie signed up for, our son Ben, and Zenzi, all of us, was that this was going to happen. Zenzi was going to take this challenge in this lifetime, and it was going to end early. As I have gone into that pain and ridden this life journey as well as I can, it has already improved my life and increased my happiness exponentially more than I could ever imagine. I love to use the Kahlil Gibran quote, 'The deeper that sorrow carves into your being, the more joy you can contain.'"

Exit Points

"When Lea was in high school, a few of her friends wanted to see a palm reader for her birthday. When I asked her what the palm reader said, she wouldn't tell me because it would be upsetting. So, I let it go. About six years prior to her passing, she was involved in a car accident in a Colorado snowstorm. She told me that she really felt like she could have died. I look at the timing of her passing, everyone she touched, and the way she lived her life. She loved her life. It was more meaningful for her to pass when she did than earlier; she chose a time when it had the greatest impact."

— Mary D, Lea's mom

The term 'exit points' refers to the concept that individuals – before they incarnate into physical existence – pre-determine certain times when they may choose to depart from this earthly realm. People in spiritual and metaphysical circles often say that we can plan the timing and circumstances of passing before being born. Exit points are chosen for various reasons: fulfilling life lessons, completing missions, or facilitating spiritual growth. These exit points are not considered to be arbitrary. Rather, they are part of a larger soul plan or contract that individuals create before their incarnation.

Dolores says, "We all have a certain passing date that's planned. That's just my feeling. There was one experience that had a lot of meaning for me. The very last day Eric left the house to go to work, I walked him to the door to say goodbye and give him a kiss and hug as we always did. He walked down the two steps on our porch, then looked back at me and said goodbye a second time. I know it seems like nothing, but I noticed. He had never done that before. When we got the terrible news of his accident, my first thought was that his soul knew. Eric's second goodbye was his way of letting me know. I think his work here was done. He affected so many people and continues to do so."

Several parents communicated with their children in the afterlife and learned that they could have taken different exit points but chose the ones they did for good reasons. **Amy** explains, "In my first reading with a medium, my son said he had a later exit point but he would have suffered. In the reading, my son communicated that passing from a Fentanyl overdose was the easiest way. Brandon said, 'I basically just need to get back up there and get to work!'"

Terri recalls, "There were moments of intuition that I could feel before Rick passed. A few weeks before, I was driving and this thought came to me: 'Rick wants to go up the hill to a place where I brought all my children camping. It's a place in nature where we were happiest.' When I got this thought, I had a feeling that he had passed on, and that is where he wanted to go. I pushed the thought away and got annoyed at myself. When Rick did transition a few weeks later, I knew that's really where he wanted to go. I asked him in spirit why he survived that second overdose just to pass on a couple of months later. I felt him say to me, 'I didn't choose to go then because you wouldn't have gone on your journey. We were meant to do this together.'"

Linda shares, "When David's mental health really deteriorated, he said: 'I promise you if anything happens to me, I'll find a way to get through to you.' It took me a long while to explore any kind of meaning though. I think one of his exit points was when he was 28 years old and he took it. I believe that David is now helping a lot of people and he's now guiding me on my journey. I've heard his voice once and the feeling that I get is, 'Mum, we're together, we're a team.'"

Andrea communicated with her daughter and says, "I always expected Chloe to transition at 19 but I don't know why. She transitioned at 28. After she passed on, I asked her about it; she told me she could have left at age 19, but wanted to stay longer. We have multiple exit points and she chose a later date. I also had a premonition about her passing in another life where we were sisters. It had been a very difficult experience and I didn't properly take care of her. I told her that, in this current life, I would take care of her until her last breath. I was able to do that."

Anne-marie learned about exit points from another HPH mother. She explains, "Angela, founder of HPH Australia, said to me that the bike accident Harry had a year before his fatal crash could have been an exit point for him. I never wanted to have children but, in my mid-30s, had a dream that was incredibly emotional. It was of me breastfeeding a baby in bed. I turned on the head of a pin – I was having that child! I aligned everything in my career and life so I could do that. I do believe now in hindsight that it was Harry saying, 'You'd better get a move on woman, you're going to run out of time!' I am incredibly grateful to Harry for being present in my life for 19 years, and his role in bringing me to where I am now."

Some parents felt the exit point was just meant to be. **Kelley** says, "My belief, especially about how Aleia left, is that her frequency / energy couldn't fit in her body anymore. The exit point was the exit point."

Danny agrees. "In the year of our son's passing, there were some signs. We didn't know how to read them then. But when we look back, we think maybe it was Ethan's destiny to pass when he did."

Ana says, "Alessandro wasn't meant to be here for a long time. He was born prematurely; then, when he was 15, he had another incident where he almost passed. But we had the good fortune of having him with us for another five years. At 20, he found his exit. He was very mature — an old soul in a young body — and was not supposed to have a long earthly experience."

Antonietta felt that the day of her son's exit gave it meaning. "My son Daniel passed on my birthday and I've thought about that a lot. Why that day? It finally dawned on me that this is part of that big picture. He's making sure I know he's always connected to me."

Kerry, whose son Sam passed on believes that "We have an in-date for birth and an out-date for death. We have a lifespan that can be a few breaths to 100-plus years. I believe the timeline cannot change, but the choices you make along that timeline are your own."

Advanced Souls

"Jillian lived fully and was here for a good time, not a long time. She was very intuitive and an old soul. When

she was about four years old, she told me more than once
that she wasn't going to live to be an adult. I took her to
a counselor and they said to just go along with it. Jillian
loved old people, babies, and the underdogs. She was full
of life: she was a cheerleader, a gymnast, and had lots of
friends."

— Louise, Jillian's mom

Several parents described their children as 'old or advanced souls'. These terms describe individuals, especially children or young people, who display uncommonly high levels of maturity, wisdom, and compassion. These qualities suggest that the child's soul had already experienced numerous lifetimes of learning and growth. From this perspective, children may live a relatively short time on earth because they fulfilled their purpose or mission. They completed all they set out to do, thus their abbreviated time on earth.

Marie describes her daughter Sienna as "a very artistic and creative child. She was the eldest and looked after her sister and cousins. Sienna was very forgiving and understood flaws of adults and children. She was a pleasure to be around and had a lot to teach. I used to call her an old soul because she had this understanding about life that even challenged my own views. One day, she drew a picture of heaven; she went to a Catholic school so I expected it to be done in a Catholic way. Instead, she drew pictures of where you chose who your parents are, where you live, and what you look like. She also drew a book and said it was *The Book of Life*."

Marie continues, "Thank goodness, I video recorded all this and asked her, 'What's in *The Book of Life*?' She said, 'Mom, you don't get to read that until the end; that's where your destiny is.' She was only about seven years old. She also said, 'At school, they're talking about hell with pitchforks but they've got it wrong. Hell is not a place where you go; hell is a state of mind.'"

Rhonda believes her son Reese is an old soul. "My son passed on by suicide at age 17. He kept a notebook and wrote over 60 handwritten letters so we knew his passing was very planned. His main message to me was, 'Please hand out all these letters and let people know they can see me.' I believe that he really had a purpose on this earth and was an old soul. I think most of our kids are old souls; they just learned their lessons early. For whatever reason, this was his plan. That gives me comfort; it's the way it was meant to be."

Christiane feels this too. "I believe in a soul plan. David transitioned at an early age because he is an old soul and accomplished what he was meant to accomplish when he was here. Unlike some parents, I try not to focus on the cancer that he had, which is hard for me because I am a cancer geneticist."

Heather states, "When my son Xavier Alexander was born, the first thing the doctor said when he handed him to me was, 'Oh he's cute!' At that moment, Xavier picked up his head and just looked at me. We started calling him Benjamin Button because he stared through us like he had such an old soul. Xavier crossed over at five months of age from SIDS. I recall never being able to picture him as a grown-up, or even reaching age five or 10. It didn't scare me, but it stuck with me. At his service, I had a shaman drumming. I wasn't a practicing shaman then, but I needed those beats to help me walk forward again."

Although some parents did not specifically call their child an 'old soul', they described them as wise beyond their years. **Warren** describes his son Nolan: "Most of our life with Nolan, there were a lot of times where we were like, 'How is he doing this?' We saw him perform songs that neither of us saw him rehearse. We're certain that he's been here before and even done the whole fame thing. I'm learning to be comfortable in the things I don't understand. To stay open is really important."

Frode says about his son, "There was always something special / different about Alexander. It was like he was in a hurry. He used to say, 'YOLO: You Only Live Once'. A couple of months after the accident, we got a voice recording of his from his school. It was a project to make a speech and the topic he picked was 'Life and Death'. He pointed out the importance of doing joyful things in life and encouraged others to call their parents and tell them they love them. At the end he said, 'Follow your dreams and don't take anything for granted. No one lives forever, not even you.'"

Carre describes her son's words after he passed on: "He came through a medium and said, 'I came here to be a bright light and shine my light as brightly as I possibly could. It's hard to maintain that level of brightness and I wanted to leave before I started to dim.'"

Chapter 4: Sharing What We Have Learned

by Anne-marie Taplin

For the Shining Light Parents who were interviewed, their child still being present is a lived reality. Their unique journeys have helped them realize, with wonder and relief, that their child has survived in a different form. Mystical experiences of these parents have comforted them and confirmed their signs of connection and love from 'across the veil'.

Many parents want to share their hard-earned insights and hope with others. In this chapter, parents answered the question: *'What are some things you've learned that you would like to share with others?'*

Parents new to the healing journey may focus a lot on the absence of their child's physical presence. Understandably, they deeply long to hear their child's voice and feel the touch of their embrace. However, as Shining Light mom Kate said so eloquently, 'Focusing on the loss only keeps us in deep grief.'

As much as possible, it's vital to recall all the love, memories, and experiences that will live in your heart and mind forever. It's important to know that each person in your child's life will remember something special. Knowing that you will see your child again – and can enjoy a beautiful relationship now – is an invaluable aid. In this chapter, Shining Light Parents who contributed to this book teach you how to do that.

We are universally bound by the love we feel for our children. One of the beautiful aspects of Helping Parents Heal as a global community is the shared intention that every topic of afterlife connection is encouraged. You can feel at ease discussing signs, vivid dreams, validating experiences with a medium, and more. You can share the surprise and joy this brought you. Together, we can more fully embrace that our children live on.

Lisa A says we don't have to "wish our life away until we transition to spirit to see our children. I see Derek without my physical eyes now and call him my 'Helen Keller child'. You just have to learn to communicate differently. A big awakening for me is that my son and I are now in a 'soul-ship' instead of a relationship. Talk about your children in the *present tense*. We've been programmed to believe a transition to spirit means *gone* but, in reality, we're still parents to our children. They are still here."

Patti, Adam's mom, believes that the healing starts with the connection with our children. "Our children want to connect with us. We all get signs from our children, so look for them, which is a type of connection, and dreams. We're not separate. There's an old-fashioned way of looking at it, that 'They're gone and I'll never see them again'. But you will see them again and can now in different ways."

Joseph's mom **Jean** says that the biggest thing is to be willing to step outside the norm and know that your love never dies. "How can it die?" she asks. "If anything, it gets stronger and purer. I'm sure you miss the physical presence, but there's an entire new relationship and a whole new world out there. And your child is ready to walk it with you, to discover this new way to live."

Anni, Anthony's mom, says, "It's so powerful to know that your child lives on. It's like a lighthouse into the abyss of the grief. It's so easy to connect heart to heart, to put your hand on your heart, and slow down your breathing."

Kyle's mom **Carol K** shares, "One thing I wish that parents would understand deeply is that their child is still there. Some parents you can help, and some you just hope that they will come to understand. I'd like parents to know that even when you tell your highest truth, *not everybody is going to get it*, or appreciate or agree with it. You may want to be discerning about who you share with."

Melissa, who passed suddenly at 18, is still cherished by her mom **Patricia**. "There are no coincidences. Don't ever dismiss contacts as that – they are signs. Thank your kid, because they really want to stay connected with you. They want you to wake up and realize they are still with you."

Andy B, Joshua's dad, says that our relationship with our children is not over – it's just in a different form. "Yes, it is challenging. It is not easy. It doesn't come without effort, but we have the potential for a totally different relationship."

Tom M, Kevin's dad, says, "Our children are not gone, they're just different."

Rick is still very much present for **Terri**. She says, "Have faith and trust that our children are here. Just because we don't see them anymore doesn't mean they're not here. Have patience. If we're too much in a rush to control how things are going to unfold, we're going to miss the gifts along the way. There are always blessings. Give yourself permission to breathe. When that grief starts to soften, you can give yourself permission to heal. I was consciously sabotaging and holding myself back, because there was guilt there. But I was ready to shift. I know Rick struggled here, and I know he is happy where he is. So I consciously decided to allow myself to heal and let it all go."

Knowing that our children live on, however, isn't always clear sailing. We all have bad days and times when we struggle. **Kerry** offers some sage advice. "It comes back to not doubting the senses you're feeling as a parent. They can only do so much to try and get your attention, so we have to help them as well. Don't dismiss those signs of your child working through pure energy to let you know 'I live on, I am here.' I also think it's important to celebrate their life. I'm so saddened when I hear of people who don't talk about their kids anymore. We've got Sam's 31st birthday coming up next month; these events are getting bigger every year, not smaller."

Antoinetta says, "I think we all have different mantras to live by to help us through. One of mine is to *make Daniel proud*. We will be with our kids again, but until then, we can be their mom or dad *from this side*. It's different. It's not the way you're used to doing it, but we are still their parents."

Kate, whose son Warren changed worlds, agrees: "The most important thing is to know we don't lose them, only their human form. I don't talk much about soul contracts to people early on because it's a lot to grasp. I realize now that I was in spirit when I chose this plan. If I had been human, I wouldn't have chosen to experience the pain."

Pat states, "Your children are there with you, they didn't die. So many people feel that they're no longer around, but that's not true at all. Children go off to college, children get married and move away. Children passing on is just another way that they leave us, but they *don't really* leave us. I even feel that they're *closer* to us after transitioning to spirit than if they moved away. We can beckon them any time we want. Tyler and I had a soul contract that we decided before we came here."

Luke's mom **Heather S** believes that riding out the difficult times is how we survive. "This journey is like being on a boat on a river. Sometimes the river is nice and smooth; you're having a good time and it's easy. But sometimes another boat comes along, and there's a wake and the water gets all choppy. You just have to ride it out." She continues, "I was raised with a lot of religious dogma, but I know God loves me and we have a direct connection to Him. It's our birthright, just as it's our birthright to be able to connect to the other side with our loved ones. We all have this gift. If I can do it, anyone can do it."

Shining Light Parents delight in hearing about signs, dreams and contact with children who have changed worlds. **Elizabeth Boisson** says: "You can connect with a pendulum, with meditation, or while walking in nature. For a year after Morgan transitioned to Spirit, I went to the top of every single mountain around my house because I felt that was really important. I felt like he was with me the whole way. There are so many ways they try to show us they're here with us."

Andrea believes that it's important to quiet the mind, even for only five minutes a day. "Cultivate the habit of getting still. We don't have all the answers from our usual perspective; we're not seeing the bigger picture. Chloe said, 'Mom, if you knew how much we are around, you'd be bumping into us all the time.'"

Anne-marie believes that our children live on. "I don't describe it as a belief system; I think it is *a knowing*. I've had too much evidence since Harry's transition to doubt that."

Judith, Carly's aunt, believes that our children are our spiritual teachers. "When they pass, they're teaching us to improve our perspective, and remember what's important in life. It's not the worldly things but our connection with love. You can develop a new relationship with your child. It's not a physical relationship anymore but that doesn't mean they're gone."

David's mom **Christiane** says that our children are not dead in the sense that we use that word. "Their souls are alive and vibrant; they're just not in *their human suit* anymore. We need to focus on the life they lived here, and not on just the day they transitioned to spirit. Try different ways that can help you shift: journaling, looking for signs, talking to other parents, sound bath healings, or meditation. Be open."

Tava, Christina's mom, believes that being open to acceptance is the first step. "Just accept any sense you get that your child is with you. Accepting that *is* your child opens the channels more and more."

This theme is echoed by **Marc**, Zenzi's dad: "Trust is number one, that our children are still right here. And not just our children; my father, ancestors, and guides are all right here with me. This gives me the presence and reassurance to transcend this grief. My brain made the pain seem so big and nasty. It was never as dark and scary as I made it out to be. The rewards of really knowing have been exponential."

Jeff C firmly believes in the importance of keeping your child in the present. "Include them in everything. Say their name. Talk to them out loud. Our kids are still with us and can experience what we're going through. Our daughter Baylee sat in with us during one of our readings with a medium, and Austin kept talking about this pair of earrings. My wife and I tried to play it down because she was just about to graduate from high school and we bought her a pair of diamond earrings. The medium said, 'No, we have to go back to the earrings.' We finally had to tell Baylee."

Truc-Co says that she'd like other parents to know that a relationship with their child 'on the other side' is possible. "You just have to find new ways to communicate with them. In our family, we incorporate Ailee in everything we do every day. We say her name freely and talk to her. We don't feel weird about it."

Paige says, "You still have a connection with your child. That's what I learned three weeks after Brian passed. I was lying awake on my bed and heard him call out loud 'Mom!' I jumped up and I said, 'I will find you, and I will not stop until I find you!' I've never stopped and never looked back. I encourage all parents to make that commitment: find your beloved child in spirit and don't stop until you do, because they are waiting for you."

Early Grief... It Does Get Easier

"My son Garrett said, 'Mom, don't keep going over and over how I passed like a hamster in a wheel turning 300 times. I didn't pass on 300 times. It's not important to me. I want to be remembered for how we laughed and how I made you laugh – not how I died.' It's easy to get stuck in the sadness, but they want us to think of happy moments."

— Laurie, Garrett's mom

None of us would ever choose to go through early grief again. We all remember the disbelief, anguish, tears and numbness and are glad to at least partly move past it. However, some grieving parents become stuck at this stage; no matter how hard they try, they feel mired in despair. Shining Light Parents demonstrate that there is *a softer and more soulful way forward*. Deep and prolonged suffering does not mean that you love your child more. Mourning forever does not prove your adoration, nor does feeling joyful again mean that you love your child less. All life is precious and so is your life.

Nicolas' mom **Paola** says we need to have tools to handle grief. "If we have some tools, we can recover from that initial moment. Be nice to yourself; with time, you can understand it is your own personal journey."

Angela L explains her journey. "We're stepping forward, now. When it first happened, we were stuck for many years. I now understand that we're all connected. I know now that bodily death is not final. I'm looking forward to moving into that space where Ethan is – *where there's no fear*. For newly grieving parents, it can be a 'breath by breath' and slow process. Four years on this path, we are healing. We know that we may never completely heal, but we're able to carry that pain in a different way."

Moving forward with grace and acceptance may feel like such an impossible dream for parents with children who recently transitioned from this earthly experience. "Grief is physically painful," says **Louise**. "As a nurse, I see a lot of Broken Heart Syndrome. It actually exists, so self-care is huge. If you can find a 'grief buddy' who'll call and ask if you've showered, for example, those little things are important. Also, we aren't keeping our kids from progressing by having them with us. That's their choice. We're not keeping them from The Light or from moving on. Jilly told me her passing was the pebble in the pond and my job is to finish the assignment."

The physical pain of early and profound grief is echoed by **Lisa H**, Shayne's mom. "I think that self-care is the hardest thing to do in the early stages of grief. It's important to do whatever you can: nap, take walks in nature, and get massages. Putting your own oxygen mask on first is critical."

Ana shares her thoughts: "This is your journey; it's about *your* steps and *your* growth. It's *your* grief too. You can say to yourself, 'I went through that door of hell'. Then you can look at yourself now and see how you've become a better person. You can become so clear from the moment they transition. You become clear from the grief and evolve."

Cindy, Josh's mom, has sound advice for newly grieving parents. "I want everybody to say this to themselves, 'You are not your grief. *You are not your grief.*' We get so consumed by it to the point where we're under water. I had a moment where I was driving down the street in the middle of nowhere, screaming my head off for five full minutes. So I understand deep grief, but it is not *who* you are; it's what you're experiencing. We were chosen to be Shining Light Parents because *we have the capability to grow from it*."

She continues, "We may say that we can't smile because feeling joy is being disrespectful to our child – but that's not true. As you grow, the joy comes around. As you're walking through life, you're still feeling some grief, but you're also expanding with joy. It's a great balance to walk through life and say, 'Yes, I know the pain but I also have this joy. I can grow, help others, and celebrate.'"

111

Finding the right tools and support is key for healing and moving forward after your child passes on. Ross's mom **Cathy** says it's critical to find that as soon as you can. "I did as much reading as I could about the afterlife because I knew my son wasn't gone. I needed to figure out where he was and how to keep that communication going. Take really good care of yourself, especially that first year, because grief is exhausting. Eat healthfully, walk in nature, and get plenty of rest. I had to pare everything down to the barest essentials. I didn't want noise and couldn't even listen to music for about two and a half years. It was like my body was *numb* and just needed to focus on healing. I surrounded myself with a few supportive and positive friends. When I found signs, they didn't make fun of me or say 'Oh, that's just a feather.'"

Every Shining Light Parent has been through the dark night of the soul. We have felt too shattered to work, cook, socialize, and sometimes even to move. **Elizabeth** speaks to this point when she says: "It's important to work towards raising our vibrations in different ways, especially being in nature. Our kids connect with us in those higher energies. I believe that when we sleep, we spend time with our kids even if we don't remember when we wake up."

Colleen says it's okay to ask for help. "That can mean attending HPH groups, or seeing a therapist or spiritual advisor. Don't be afraid to ask for help. Be sure to talk about your child; it may make people uncomfortable but that's okay. I talk about my son Denis a lot. My life has completely changed. I'm no longer working full time in a corporation; I am serving and helping others, so it's a blessing."

Joanna's son Peter told her that newly grieving parents can anticipate and get over some of the hurdles before they actually happen. She describes his input: "First, wrap yourself in the love and focus on your needs one breath at a time. Continue to talk to your loved one; open a simple dialogue in whatever way feels natural to you. Second, know that everybody grieves differently. This will mean that friends and family may not respond as you do, and that may not be easy. Third, keep your mind completely open and question everything you have ever thought to be true. We are all capable of much more than we think."

The advice of choosing who you are around during early grieving is echoed by **Linda R**. "If I had known back then what I know now, it would have been a lot easier after Chris passed. All you have to do is believe in yourself and choose your friends wisely."

Trusting your feelings and grieving in your own way are other common threads in these interviews. **Pamela** explains: "Don't worry about people who say *you should do this,* or *you shouldn't do that.* Not long after my daughter Michele crossed over, someone told me I should pack up and get rid of all of her things. Five years later, her room is the same. I didn't get rid of her clothes; in fact, I wear them. Do what you feel is right for you."

Two Shining Light dads agree with the 'you being you' approach during grief. **Mike** says there are no rules while deeply mourning. "Even spouses need to realize that we're all on different points of our grief timeline. Above all else, acceptance and patience are the keys to realizing that we don't have to understand what's happened. When I finally embraced that, I actually began to heal after Dylan passed on."

Chris shares, "It's okay to ask big, tough, gnarly questions. It's fine to go through all the things that you need to go through. Accept being shaken to the core, being shattered, and putting yourself back together one day at a time."

Kelley says it's very helpful to honor *all* sides of grief. "This includes physical grief, cellular grief, and spiritual grief. I see parents get stuck in one or the other; they may immediately go into the spiritual side of grief, but there's a *physical* side that has to be addressed as well. I encourage parents to recognize and allow both. Be a mess as long as you need to. Allow yourself to consider 'I literally feel like my DNA changed the day Aleia passed on.' I have absolutely embraced every aspect of that."

"I wish more people were okay with feeling their feelings," says **Warren**, Nolan's dad. "The dads who come to the HPH Fathers Group are still trying to do the programming of being stoic and strong. They quickly learn that it doesn't work. Then they open to all kinds of help redefining what it means to be a man. That means being vulnerable, kind, loving, and surrendering – letting others help you."

Candi, whose son James changed worlds, says we have to learn to put ourselves first. "As moms, we're used to putting everybody else first. But, especially when you're in early grief, you need to put yourself first and be kind of selfish. Even though our lives won't be the same again, we can focus on ourselves more. Our kids can help guide us with that."

Sophia, Xander's mom, says: "Try to be okay with your emotions and be sure to regularly process your grief. Stuffing it inside, trying to stay busy, or allowing it to be stuck in your body will not help in the long run. You can feel happy one minute, and the next you're having a breakdown. Feel it and process it. Give yourself a few minutes –

ten minutes is what I did for myself after Xander passed on – and then get moving."

David says, "The hardest thing I had to deal with initially was acceptance that my children Ginger and Tracy had passed on. The second year was almost harder because I was coming to terms with the reality of it. When I feel Ginger around me, it's not strong enough – it's not what I want. But it's better than what I would have experienced had I not gone through the process of awakening."

Ann G, whose sons Matthew and Scott graduated from earth school, wants parents to know that hope and healing are possible. "I've heard many times, *if you don't have hope now, we'll hold it for you until you can find it.* That is so powerful. Be gentle with yourself. I was trying to control my grief and had to learn to *let my grief lead me* through self-compassion, learning to say 'no', and who can I talk to."

"You're deep in grief during the first few years," says **Michelle T**. "After Jordan passed, I had a hard time reading because my eyes were swollen from crying. I saw Suzanne Giesemann speak at a retreat and, on the way there, we were reading Robert Schwartz's book *Your Soul's Plan*. What I learned from them was like a light bulb going off. It got me through the dark night of the soul and still helps me today."

Judith explains: "I hope everyone knows that the shock of what happened, the acute stress you experienced, is real. Without help, it can keep you stuck in post-traumatic stress syndrome for the rest of your life. Once the trauma is lifted though, it can be healed – it's not a life sentence."

Helpful Tips for Newly Grieving Moms and Dads

When we just focus on one side of the dualities in life –
just yin but not yang, just sadness but not joy – our grief
journey can be so hard. Don't make it a mutually
exclusive thing: leave some room for laughter and
happiness during the grief."

— Louis, Joe's dad

Lin believes that seeing a more positive angle is significant. "Human beings are meaning-making machines; something happens, and we give meaning to it. Early on, I got so upset when I would get letters addressed to Ryan at my house. *Why are people sending these? Don't they know he died?* Then I 'flipped the switch' and intentionally turned it into a positive. Now, instead of getting upset, I call it a 'Godwink' – a hello from heaven. I kiss the letter, toss it away, and don't feel any self-perpetuated pain. I know it's really tough early on, but 'flipping the switch' can be helpful."

Xavier's mom **Heather H** suggests that we trust that small, still voice within. "It seems so simple to just be still. You think you have this world of problems, but just take that five minutes. We all have five minutes, regardless of how busy we are. Take that time and surrender; it just opens you up and makes life a little more bearable in that moment."

Chris' mom **Merle** shares, "Our children have just moved into the next phase of life; it's right here. I know it's hard to be happy, especially in the beginning. But I want people to know they can feel happy – they're allowed to feel joy and laugh. Their kids are cheering when they do that and celebrate lives. As hard as it may seem, look ahead – not at what you've lost. Don't focus on missing your physical child; develop a relationship with your children where they are now. They want a relationship with you, so work towards that."

Frode encourages, "Try to include your child in your everyday life. Talk about them. Travel with them. We always bring a rock with Alexander's name on it when we go somewhere new, and place it out in the open. Know your child is always with you, no matter what."

Anna agrees: "I always ask Alexander questions: *What do you think about this? What should I do?* Then I sit and listen, and usually it comes in really quickly. I can hear an answer that is similar to a thought. We've been going through some rough times with the investigations and trials; he tells me 'Let it go.' That's been so helpful. *Let it go.* Just do those three words."

Recommendations

"Don't be afraid to feel all your feelings. Explore different ways to raise your own vibrational frequency. For me, that includes sound baths, conscious breathwork sessions, time in nature, and listening to birds singing. Being at one with the environment helps to raise your energy levels. It's helped my connection with my boy. Surrender to being present and still in the moment."
— Linda O, David's mom

"I started straight away with meditation and now yoga has become a big part of my life," says **Angela B**. "I do development classes at my local spiritualist church and Erin connects very much in signs. I received a Christmas present with a sunflower, which represented her, but I was more excited by the box because it has a little angel on it and inside it says 'keep on' – a phrase we connect with her."

Dolores says that if you set the intention to heal, you will. In contrast, "I knew from the beginning after Eric passed that I was going to figure this out. Healing is a lifelong journey. It's not like one day I'm going to wake up and know I'm done healing. This journey will continue to evolve. Along the way I've learned that grief and joy can coexist. I didn't believe that was possible in the beginning."

At three-and-a half-years in, **Wendy** is filled with gratitude and joy. "I've received so much evidence that he is walking this path with me. I am deeply committed to living my best life for him because I know he's watching. He wants that for me and I want that for myself. It's possible. Initially, I saw grief as an adversary, a thing that I needed to get through, but I realize that *grief is healing*. It's a part of the human experience, and it's very important to get support for that. Grief and joy are both part of my emotional wheelhouse. Yes, I still cry a couple times a week, and never know when the grief bomb is going to hit. But I also feel truly joyful in moments that I know my son Hugh has led me to."

"It takes work, but you can survive the passing of a child," says **Ty**. "I've always been a reader, a member of a book club for 20-plus years. The first year after Shayna passed on, I lost track of how many books I read, videos I watched, and podcasts I listened to. *You can survive the loss* and find joy again. I'm not the same person that I was – I'm a different version of me."

Kathy says you won't always feel the way you feel right now. "This is a *changing* experience. Don't listen too closely to other people's experiences because sometimes they won't share the most positive things with you. Don't automatically take their words to heart because everyone's journey is unique. You are being guided and led to your kindred-spirit group, your tribe. Trust your kids to get you there. I realize now that grief and joy can occupy the exact same space at the exact same time."

According to **Carolyn**, Cara's mom, hope is a big key. "It's very hard to find hope at the beginning, but listening to parents like us can give you hope that *you can get there*. Even though you may not be able to feel your children or communicate with them yet, you will get there."

Weston's mom **Galen** believes that being okay with vulnerability is also vital. "Be open to learning. For me I believe this is the key towards finding peace."

Andy B suggests, "Get quiet and go deep inside whether it's through meditation, running, bike riding, or yoga. When you get inside yourself, you stop thinking and then you can hear. I talk to my son every day. I don't hear Joshua reply audibly, but I get very strong impressions of him answering my questions."

You Can Find Joy and Live Again

"I didn't want to be that person everybody looked at and felt sorry for. I didn't want to be the face of sadness. I just couldn't be that. HPH helped me be a Shining Light Parent – to let my son shine through me, do good things and feel joy."

— Allison, mother of Davey

Elizabeth Boisson has a powerful saying that shows how to heal your pain and suffering. "It's important to look for the 'collateral beauty' because this journey is not all sad." Shining Light Parents share what this means in their daily life after their child – or, in some cases, children – change worlds.

Conrado says that what matters most is finding joy in life again: "I'm not talking about joy like when you're on a fast roller coaster with your hands up. I'm talking about the joy of being able to look at a sunrise and feel that magic. Looking at a photograph of your child and remembering that moment. These and other things bring more happiness."

Nancy, Will and Joey's mom, agrees: "It's possible to live through this and find yourself past the deep pain. It's possible to find joy again, it really and truly is. Although it may be difficult – especially in the beginning – let go of sadness and constantly trying to remember them in the physical. Let yourself feel joy again and smile. It's not going to diminish your connection with them because that connection is unbreakable."

You'll hear a lot about 'joy' in Helping Parents Heal circles, but what does it mean? Shining Light Parents suggest focusing on *every joy* – gratitude, appreciation, wonder, creativity, and more – that raises your vibration. When you upgrade your energy, you improve how you feel and your emotions.

Bill V explains: "I woke up at 5:30 this morning and laid there trying to get back to sleep. Suddenly I saw purple, yellow, and green lights come into the room. I was enveloped in it and thought 'Wow, Greg's here. He obviously wants to talk.' I wrote down what I heard:

'We know there is a deep loss when you 'lose' a child in the physical. We also know there is a universal law that what you think and feel manifests in what you create. We are eternal so it makes sense that after a loss we move forward to acceptance of the loss, for that cannot be altered. This acceptance leads to a higher vibration of thinking and feelings. This higher vibration aids being able to connect and have a relationship with our departed child on the other side until we are again reunited with our child and all our departed loved ones. It's beautiful, we never die. Think of your child as being on vacation in a better place until you meet up again.'"

Susan, Bill's wife, expands on this message: "Greg talks to his dad and to me through his dad about the absolute importance of parents finding happiness and joy again. We did not come to earth to be miserable; in fact, the opposite is true. Greg says, 'It is no small matter, but you have to move through it, accept it and try to make something positive out of what has happened to you.'"

Jordan's mom **Barb** agrees that we don't need to suffer: "Our culture says we have to suffer, but I experience joy. I go out to dance and love walking in nature. It gives me so much connection. Celebrate when you're smiling and feeling better. That's what our children want us to do. I celebrate the times when I feel good. It's not all the time, but I rejoice when it happens because there's nothing better."

Amber inspired her mom **Lisa L** to live fully on earth while she can. "One thing that helped me early on was imagining if I had passed and Amber was left behind. Would I want her lamenting and saying 'I'll never move on'? Or would I want her to heal, develop a different kind of relationship with me, and have a beautiful life helping people? That's what I'd want for her, so that's what she'd want for me."

Anne-marie's frequent experience of grief is leading to a state of acceptance and calm. "Grief doesn't always have to be heavy and joyless. I know that Harry is somewhere, that he does live on. I often feel intensely curious about what Harry is doing and I have had some good communication around that."

Annie encourages parents to work with each other in this grief journey. "It's really helped me so much to have that common language. Also, remember we're still on earth for good reasons even though our children aren't living on earth as before. With intention and purpose, you will feel more like yourself again. It just takes some time."

Find Your Kindred Spirits

"Eventually, we found people who share joy and amazement in our story; these are the people we hang around with. When we get together, the first questions out of their mouths are, 'What's Devon up to? What have you heard from Devon lately?' When you have your crew – your kindred spirits – around, it's easier to get to a place of joy.

— Jeff H, Devon's dad

Chandra firmly believes that knowing you are not alone is vital. "The sense of isolation is massive and it continues because people are often not comfortable talking about grief and loss. That can be even more so when your child passes on. Our children have moved to a different plane, one that we don't know much about. But we can still connect and learn and read about it. We won't experience it till we go there ourselves, but we are learning here and our children are learning on the other side."

Emma says, "Finding your tribe is really important. Find people who understand and know that connection with our kids is possible. Try different things in your journey of healing."

Jeff C shares, "You're not alone. There are moms, dads, so many of us out there with similar stories who are willing to help." Another HPH Fathers' Group member, **Chris M**, says that group is "a safe place for guys to come together."

Ty encourages, 'Don't think you have to grieve alone. Finding groups like HPH with other parents who are going through the same thing really helps."

Ann G elaborates: "Grief can be isolating. There's no right or wrong way to grieve. We all have to figure out what works for us, but connection is really important. Grief is exhausting, it's overwhelming, but it does ease over time."

Megan says that having others to walk the journey with softens grief's edges. "We all deserve someone to hold our hand. No matter how long you've been on this journey, you have something to give to others, even if it doesn't feel that way. There's no separation with our kids. I like to imagine we're bonded to our kids with ribbons of love carried by light."

Anne-marie: "We can transform ourselves and heal – not in a sense of 'moving on', but moving forward. Also, we need to find our tribe because they can save us." (To learn more about how to find kindred spirits and expand your support circle, see article #66 at SoulProof.com and Resources in Appendix C)

Chris R says: "It's important for parents to find people who are there for you. It may not be the people you expect since family is sometimes not very available. I like to bring Sean's name into a conversation. I try not to be afraid of how other people are going to react when I talk about my son. I don't bring him up casually; I do it with intention to find people who are going to be there for me."

Sandra, Josh's mom, agrees, "It's not the kind of journey we should do alone. We need the support of others who understand. It's so important to surround yourself with the right people."

Lea's mom **Mary D** shares: "Although we're all connected, this is an individual journey. Choose what works best for you and connect with like-minded people. Don't suppress your feelings – acknowledge them. Breathe them in and let go of what doesn't serve you. I think so many times we try to suppress our feelings: 'I don't want to go there, I don't want to cry, I don't want to get upset.' Just let it come and let it go. We need to be in touch with those common human feelings."

Helping others is a common theme among Shining Light Parents. As we become stronger, there is often a deep urge to communicate what we have learned and ease the burden of other moms and dads.

Beverly knew her way of healing would be to help and be of service to other parents. "I didn't want to be in the 'bereaved parents club' after Mason passed. Instead, I asked 'What can I do with the worst that has happened? How can I make it better?' I've learned that you can't cocoon yourself for too long. Our children guide us to find and help others."

Andy believes that men often believe they have to carry all the pain by themselves. "Men love to isolate. We tend to use drinking and drugs to divert our pain, and be strong for those that we love. In reality, we're showing weakness by not being vulnerable, not sharing our emotions, and not being close with those around us."

Elizabeth reinforces what many parents eventually learn: "It's so important to find your people because, unfortunately, a lot of times family and friends just don't understand. When we start to talk about our kids, they try to change the subject. Gravitate to people who are listening and excited, not the ones saying: 'You really need to get over this, to stop thinking about your child.'"

Afterlife Connections

"Your child is with you more than you know. The signs and synchronicities are real so be open to and acknowledge them. Allow your child to help you see this life through a different lens and focus on new possibilities. Trust and surrender to it."

— Christine, Andrew's mom

Afterlife connections are sometimes the difference between living with hope and positivity versus struggling. Parents in HPH benefit from openly discussing signs, dreams, and other forms of afterlife communication. This is a crucial part of bonding and healing.

Lynn has learned that connections help her sense her son Devon better. "You can connect in nature while walking, bike riding, animals, or gardening – connecting with the earth is very healing. There's a wonderful connection through HPH with opportunities to connect via online, Facebook, and in-person. However you connect, it's a blessing."

She continues, "I've also learned that sometimes you have to give up your old way of thinking to allow miracles to happen. You might lose some friends along the way and that's okay. Our daughter has had a hard time coming along on this journey with us after her brother passed on. That's been a challenge. But it's opened up space for new people to come into our life. Be open to miracles; they're out there every day and can bring you joy and laughter."

Renee, Zack's mom, knows the power of signs from beloved children who have transitioned from earth. "I know a parent whose child transitioned 21 years ago, but she wasn't seeing any signs. I was able to teach her how to ask for them and what to look for. Soon after, she called me to say she received her first sign! I told her this wasn't the first sign sent to her; she simply figured out how to recognize and receive it. I hope more parents can learn, grow, and recognize signs from their kids like I have."

When you're not sure, **Carre** has some great advice. "If you think that maybe it's a sign, go ahead and say thank you, just in case. Because the more you thank and recognize them, the more signs you'll get. Just try to stay up and ride the waves instead of getting taken under."

David A also says that thanking your child for a sign is an important acknowledgement. "It's no different than when your child was a little kid and came to you with a drawing they did in school. If you just say, 'Oh that's nice' and throw it away, that's sad. But if you proudly display it on the fridge, point to it, and say, 'Look at this!' It's almost the same when they communicate with you now. Expressing gratitude opens up more of that."

Ramona agrees: "Acknowledge the signs. Some moms ask how to know the sign is from their child. If it feels like it warms your heart, it's likely a sign from your child. Others might say, 'How do you know it's not just a coincidence?' It's still meaningful whether it is a coincidence, synchronicity, or can be explained by science. Children in the next realm have to work with what we have on earth: license plates that already exist or butterflies that are already here."

She continues, ""We were going to one of Mia's sisters' birthday party. Family members from three cars were gathering to go inside when I noticed the car parked next to us. The license plate was 'UNA MIA': 'the one Mia'. Some people might call it a coincidence, but for me that was a complete confirmation that she was there. Acknowledge the signs and say thank you."

Pamela shares what she has learned after her daughter Michele changed worlds, "They're still right here; they haven't gone away. They haven't gone away to a far-off place; they're around us — at least part of the time. They're in our lives and can see what's going on. We can learn to communicate with them and continue that relationship."

Rhonda says, "To them, an earthly year is short — maybe like a doctor's appointment. Even a long human life is only like a blink of an eye to them. Our children are always around us if we need them."

Sherry tells an inspiring story about communication with Gabriel: "After the miscarriage with him, I had five very close family members transition to spirit. I also became very involved with end-of-this-life care for my dad. Something very special happened right after he passed on. I was sitting at the foot of his bed and outwardly heard a soft, gentle voice speak a few words in Arabic. They translated to 'Don't worry about Dad.' That was a gift. A few days later, I began to feel his presence strongly."

Sherry continues, "His communications were remarkable; for example, he helped me find legal documents and do some repairs that I would never know how to do. I share this because, if you fear that your child passed on alone, I can assure you they did not. Knowing this and releasing fear can help you enjoy ongoing communication now."

Mary reminds us that this communication takes effort and commitment. "You need to regularly connect through the pathway from *your* heart to *their* heart. You have to work at it to some extent. The reason why we're not hearing them is usually us. Two things can make a big difference. First, ask for help; counselors, teachers, and others can help you make that connection. Second, don't have expectations that you're going to hear from your child in a certain way since it's different for everyone."

Rosanne says: "Your child's personality doesn't change when they cross over. If your child was quiet and introspective while on earth, they might not come through like gangbusters. Their communications might be very subtle. My advice is to try different healing modalities and resources; dive deep and find what works for you and your child."

Sue, mom to Austin and Kyle, shares: "I absolutely believe that our children can hear us and that we can communicate. I have had success with writing a letter to them. Then I get relaxed, turn the page, and write a letter from them to me."

Sara: "Look for what resonates with you. Pay attention to something that opens up your heart or stays with you for a while. I love the word *resonate* and feel that's our children saying, 'Hey, we're on the same page with this word or thought.' Also, remember that *love really is forever.* I thought Scott would be gone in maybe three years after he changed worlds. But it's been 30 years and he's never left me. This is an eternal relationship, not just temporary until they leave to do something else. He is present with me all the time, now more than ever. So keep your hearts open to all of that, and give yourself time."

Marla: "Try to get out of the thinking, rational part of your brain – the data-driven part – that tells you you're making it all up. Open to your higher self and clearly focus your thinking on compassion, openness, and gratitude."

Personal Growth

"The pain is purposeful; it's frightening to start with, but it's transformative. There are many dark nights of the soul where you feel the level of pain might become unmanageable. For me, the pain has been part of the transformation to where I am now and seeing the bigger picture. It's brought us into contact with some amazing people and has extended our family."

— Danny, Ethan's dad

Finding meaning may be the biggest challenge for parents whose child left *seemingly* early. We may find meaning through religious / spiritual world views, and evidence for soul planning. We can create meaning through the way we live after our children pass on. A lot of parents talk about 'honoring' their child; that can mean different things to different people. For some, honoring their child means moving forward, finding joy every day, and helping others. It can mean actively creating something beautiful, or expressing emotions and memories through art or writing. Some parents honor their child with a special monument, event, or charity.

In contrast, some parents believe that they dishonor their 'lost' child if they deviate from the path of prolonged misery and acute grief. Of this, **Tom** says: "Don't get stuck in grief; you have to vent it. Cry in the fetal position, beat a punching bag, hit golf balls, or whatever works for you... but *vent*! You're not honoring your child by holding onto the grief – that's the opposite of what they want. Parents can grow by learning to forgive themselves, doctors, Creator / Life, and those who caused the death. Forgiving ourselves is vital since many parents think they are to blame for what happened."

Janean elaborates: "This human experience is so much bigger than it seems; it's a blip in time. Try to think about it that way, even just for a few minutes, and take yourself out of the cyclical negative pattern. I want to get everything out of the experience I came here for. I don't want to mess it up or waste a second of this journey. When I cross the finish line, I want to see Sean's face and for him to be proud of me."

The passing of a beloved child is widely acknowledged as a severe challenge that understandably causes deep grief. Even so, many parents have experienced profound spiritual growth while searching for meaning, purpose, and a soulful way forward. **Amy S** says, "Work every day at giving yourself love, acceptance, compassion, and forgiveness. Then give it to other people. With just that, you can help heal and grow."

Michelle J shares: "I'm going through a growing period right now where I have an earthly body. My kids Ben and Grace don't have that now, but they are still right here. I believe that heaven is 'here' – not way up in the sky somewhere; my children are 'here' too. I believe that we will be reunited and can come back in another incarnation with bodies."

Margaret says she doesn't often share her feelings that her son's passing was a gift. "I asked Kenny to help me with this question. He said, 'When you lean in, that's where you're closest to your child. Once you know you're not alone, that's when you'll begin to see the signs. The world becomes clear, the energy is pure, and you become highly aware of all the energy that surrounds you like a superpower. You were chosen to spread this pure energy.'"

The gift of *spiritual awakening through suffering* is a consistent theme for these parents. "I truly believe now that Mitch's passing was my trigger event," says **Maggie**. "I was such a different person back then. I have so much more compassion now. I feel like I have a mission; because of his passing, I am a HPH affiliate leader, yoga teacher, recovery specialist, and grief coach. I'm able to help people get through their toughest times, and know there can be happiness and love on the other side of grief."

Truc-Co also experienced this change of priorities. "Keep your heart open. Ailee's transition to spirit jump-started my spiritual heart. My priorities about how I want to spend the rest of my life shifted."

Bill T echoes this sentiment: "I talk to Jordan multiple times a day. There was a speaker at the HPH conference who said that *our child's passing is our greatest awakening*. The amount of growth that we've experienced and our ongoing relationship with Jordan has just been incredible."

Galen suggests that we trust that there is *more*. "Trust that love never dies and there is a much bigger plan in the works because our child left before us. This can all be unpacked with patience and conscious intention and *expecting miracles*."

"Wherever you are on your journey, it's okay. Try not to fight it," says **Lisa W**. "If you have days where you're feeling so much more vulnerable, all you really need to do is simply breathe and let things happen. Our children will help carry us through."

Andy M speaks of a permanent change in how we are now. "We knew we weren't going to return to being the same people we originally were, and that's okay. We have a different path now, a different journey, different communication. We're on that path and we're exploring it as best we can."

Chris' mom **Tammy** says, "There is a plan, a bigger picture. We just have to keep our eye on that even though that can be hard sometimes."

Rick & Beth O agree: "Stuff happens for a reason; we have been given numerous signs about that. As you begin to understand the meaning of why this happened, you may not understand it – but try to accept it. Knowing that your kids are still alive and reconnecting with them on a different level makes the whole process easier. It's not a loss; it's a *movement through*, a transition to a better state for both you and your children. So many parents have said they're actually closer now to their children than when they were on earth."

Marla says our work right now is here in the world of *form*. "My work is at the intersection of the world of spirit and the world of form. Metaphysical experiences and spiritual connections we have with our kids are so affirming. It's so important for you to *feel your grief*, to go through it, to recognize it, and mourn. But I didn't want to be in mourning for the rest of my life. I meditated and asked my guides, 'How can I be of the most help to my clients and HPH parents?' I immediately heard, 'You need to be clear on the three things that have helped you.' I wrote them down: personal responsibility, acceptance, and willingness. *Willingness* means you want to move beyond the story of your loss. You can be victimized by life, but you don't have to be a victim of it. I love the quote: 'If your story begins to change, do not be so loyal to your suffering that your healing doesn't stand a chance.'"

Moving Past What Happened

"Your relationship continues and you can create new memories with your children. There are at least two reasons for an early transition to spirit: a physical reason and a spiritual reason. As humans, we often get fixated on the physical reason – whether it is suicide, overdose, or cancer – but there's also a spiritual reason and plan."

— Tom, Ailee's dad

Often, we blame ourselves for our child's passing. Was it something we did? Was there something we could have done to save them?

What if we'd been there? What if they hadn't gone out that night? **What if? What if? What if?** No matter what your beliefs about soul planning and destiny are, none of us can go back and change the past.

Deb, Dean's mom, explains: "Probably the hardest thing for me is the guilt. Give yourself a break. I have a phrase, 'I forgive myself for not being perfect. I am living the very best way I know how.' That has really helped me."

Chris V says, "You need to realize you did everything you could to save your child. It's not your fault. I've come to know that I couldn't have prevented my son Daniel's passing. I could not have loved him anymore than I did. If love could have kept him here, he would still be here. I also believe that he wants me to be happy; he never liked it when I was upset. I try to make him proud of me, be happy, and find joy because that's what he would want for me."

Kate agrees that profound guilt is usually felt by parents whose child moves into the next phase of life by choice. "Suicide is a very complicated thing for parents because we sometimes think they chose to leave us, or we did something wrong, or missed something. I came to realize that Warren didn't really leave me; almost as soon as he passed, he showed up in the light. I didn't have to search for him. He was sensitive, socially awkward, and slow to adapt to new things – all that made high school really hard. I think he started to withdraw and took solace in playing video games. He disconnected more and more over the years. It was slow and happened right before our eyes, but we didn't really understand that he was in crisis, that he had depression. He was trying to do it on his own and he lost his way. I immediately got into mental health and suicide prevention advocacy after his passing, and I know he is working with me – we're a great team."

The advice to avoid self-blame is echoed by **Pamela**. "We take on a lot of guilt and blame when our child dies. To paraphrase Tom Zuba: 'God is the loving and divine intelligence of the universe; and God, at the perfect time, took our children Home.' We are not more powerful than God, so we need to stop going over what we could have or should have done."

Ty agrees and says, "One of the hardest things for me, after accepting that it actually happened, was letting go of self-blame. My husband Brian and I didn't do anything wrong, it wasn't our fault. We're both very different people now with different careers. Our other daughter changed her major and is helping people. And I'm not afraid of death anymore."

After a traumatic event, many people reassess their belief systems and philosophies. Experiencing a child's passing can be a huge push towards spiritual growth. Once the immediate shock and disbelief pass to some extent, parents feel motivated to investigate spiritual belief systems and research evidence for the afterlife. Many of them search for podcasts, books, films, and groups that investigate survival of consciousness.

"I've learned there is no death," says **Claudia**. "From the signs I get and the books I've read, I know our children are trying hard to get our attention. We have to stay open and meditate to raise our vibrations so we can meet somewhere in the middle. We can best sense them when we are in a good state, stay open to signs and synchronicities, and remain faithful and curious. We can find them in spirit. I continue to build my relationship with Emma."

Marie says, "I've learned from Sienna that there is more to this reality than we can understand right now. Even though it feels like we're stuck in all this pain and turmoil, there is a bigger picture for us to see. I believe there are good reasons why our children passed, even though we don't understand yet. If we stay open to knowing more, we will in the right way and time. Videos, books, and people will cross our paths and help us heal. When you feel ready to quit looking back, meaning and growth are there to be found."

Mabel knows that love is the most powerful force in the universe. "My husband and I have witnessed this as truth. Love for our son and other young people has helped us turn pain into purpose. Our purpose after Leo's passing was to help raise awareness about a vaccine that can protect kids from the strain of meningitis that infected him. Leo continues to save lives because of his exit. We cannot bring him back, but we can prevent other families from suffering."

Seeing the end of this earthly life in a new light is a theme that often emerged throughout these interviews. **Irene** shares, "Death is really just the loss of your human body. Life and love are eternal. As the medium Gordon Smith says, 'You can't die for the life of you.' There is absolutely nothing you could have done to prevent your child's passing so guilt and blame are pointless. They'll do nothing for you in your journey. Learning to live day by day and be here in the now really helps – especially for those early in grief. What has helped me a lot is realizing that *surrender does not mean giving up, it means reaching a point of acceptance* about what happened."

Greater awareness about the big picture of life conveys a multitude of benefits. These include, for example, improving how we use our remaining time on earth, choosing to help others, and loving more.

Beth and **Rick O** have moved past what happened. Jessica was nine and Josh was seven when their bodies were killed in 1999. In Rick's words, "On a Sunday afternoon, a drunk driver ran through a red light at over 80 miles an hour and broadsided our minivan. Both kids passed on within 30 minutes, but we somehow survived. When your children first cross over, you want contact with them so desperately because you need to know they're okay and safe. You need to know they're still there. For us, it's gone from that to knowing they're pulling things together for us as we move forward. They help us when we're working with other people."

Beth adds: "That is one of the biggest shifts parents can make: don't limit your children by thinking of them as helpless victims and little kids for eternity. We were blessed to have those advanced souls in our presence for years. We keep in touch with them and are so proud of what they're doing."

Chapter 5: Shining Even More Brightly!

by Mark Pitstick

We hope this book has informed, inspired, and comforted you. You now have a wealth of practical tips and insights to use daily. I suggest that you read this book again and **take notes** about action steps to improve every aspect of your life.

Parents on the journey FROM deeply grieving TO brightly shining need wise and loving counseling and teaching. You just learned a lot of that type of advice. Unfortunately, you have be careful about who you listen to; here are three examples of that...

A. Just last evening, we held an *Ask the Soul Doctor* class where parents asked questions and heard my best answers and holistic solutions. A mother shared about visiting an energy practitioner who said that she 'needs to move on' even though her daughter transitioned from earth **only four months earlier**. Further, this 'healer' said the mom's sadness was hurting her daughter in 'the spirit world'.

B. A father recently told me he went to a psychotherapist for grief counseling after his son changed worlds. The dad shared signs and visits that he was excited about, but was told he was delusional because there is no life after death. She gave him a 'failure to distinguish reality' diagnosis and recommended anti-depressant drugs.

C. A supposed grief recovery expert told people via social media that lasting and deep pain is inevitable if you really miss and love your children.

Run – don't walk – if you encounter similarly misinformed teachings. As you now know, none of their advice is true. Instead, you now understand that:

A. Everyone heals in their own way, and there is no set time frame for when a parent should 'get over it'. Your children's life and passing will always be a significant part of your life. Yes, your life has been irrevocably changed; you'll get used to your 'new normal' and appreciate silver linings. Over time, especially with intention, you can adjust your focus to: appreciating all the wonderful memories, realizing you'll see each other again, developing a different relationship now, helping others, and being positively transformed by this experience. (#41)

   Regarding the 'hurting your daughter' comment, clinical evidence indicates that, yes, children can still feel what their loved ones on earth are going through and have empathy for them. However, they are not 'hurt' in any way by their awareness of a loved one's sadness. The postmaterial children know, or are learning, how to transmute lower energy emotions into higher ones. For example, they may focus on cheering their parents on and encouraging them to remember the big picture of life.

B. Signs and visits from children who have moved into the next phase of life are very common. Over the past decade, I've spoken to thousands of HPH members and often ask: 'How many of you have experienced at least one meaningful contact with your children during the waking or dream state?' Nearly everyone raises their hand. Unfortunately, many academics and professionals are atheists (don't believe in a Higher Power) and / or nihilists (don't believe in life after death). I recommend asking potential caregivers if they are either of those. If they are, or are uncomfortable talking about those subjects, I would look elsewhere for help.

C. As discussed in Chapter 1, it simply is not true that lasting and deep pain is inevitable. You can love and miss your children greatly AND, at the same time, choose to have a great life that honors your child and blesses you and others.

Take-Aways

After each set of interviews, Lynn and I felt grateful for being in the presence of such love, strength, and wisdom. It was a sacred privilege to listen to and learn from these dear ones. These parents have gone through extremely tough challenges and are now serving others. What's more, they are often very happy, peaceful, and grateful for the lessons and silver linings they discovered. As Lynn and I compared notes months later, we discovered that we were still *in awe of their strength of spirit*.

I have earned so many important lessons from these Shining Light Parents. Here are several for each question that stand out for me:

1. Please tell us about your children's life and how they passed on.

A. So many of these 'kids' appeared to be advanced / evolved souls. Put another way, these children embodied and manifested higher energy and consciousness. The parents told such beautiful stories about their children who were exceptionally creative, thoughtful, and compassionate. The love of these children was especially evident when they interacted with babies, schoolmates who were mistreated by others, animals, and nature.

B. A significant percentage of the children had difficulty coping with how difficult and cruel it can be on earth. Many of them passed on via suicide and substance use disorders. In my clinical experience, their bodies often suffered from chemicals and toxic metals from pesticides, herbicides, excess vaccinations, and other ubiquitous sources. They also suffered from nutritional deficiencies, junk food, over-stimulation, excess electromagnetic radiation, and plastic micro-particles that acted as endocrine disruptors.

The cumulative load of these stressors sometimes led to self-medicating with drugs and alcohol. All of this sets the stage for feeling overwhelmed, developing diseases, having accidents, and poor decision making. Those who passed on via suicide or drug overdoses just couldn't handle it anymore.

(To be clear, I am not at all saying that children who passed on in these ways were at fault. I and others are trying to prevent more children from suffering similar imbalances. Many parents want to create more meaning to their children's lives by helping to identify and rectify root causes of common physical and mental ailments. To learn more about the causes and holistic solutions of these imbalances, see articles #26, 32, 33, 36, 43, 64, and my *Radiant Wellness* book)

C. At memorials and celebrations of life, parents heard firsthand reports from people whose lives were deeply touched by knowing their children: 'slow learners' and 'geeks' were befriended by these children who were popular and accomplished; doctors and nurses were amazed at pediatric cancer patients who cheered up others in the hospital; other students in need were helped by these children before they passed on. It's easy to conclude that, indeed, these special kids had finished – or never really needed – earth school.

HOW your child passed on was simply their ticket back Home, their 'off ramp' into the next stage of life. We hope this book helps you honor their lives while on earth AND be excited about what they are doing now.

2. How did you discover Helping Parents Heal (HPH) and how did that help you?

A. In response to the first part of this question, a surprising number of parents answered, 'I don't know, it just happened'. Magically synchronistic and serendipitous events brought them to this wonderful organization. Some parents were told by their 'deceased' children via waking or dream messages to join HPH.

B. Parents healed and transformed the most when they 'dived into' the various resources available at HPH. They made it a mission to learn more about the afterlife and what their children might be experiencing. Parents explored how to continue relationships with their children who were no longer living on earth. Several verbalized: 'I HAD to get in touch with my child and continue our loving connection'.

C. Some parents shared that they felt anxious about asking for help. This is understandable, especially for those who take pride in being independent, but please reach out for help when you need it. You're not being a bother since HPH helpers get so much joy and meaning out of being there when needed. As one group leader said, 'Our motto is: if you can't walk, we'll carry you until you can again'.

3. How are you now serving others through HPH, and what motivated you to do that?

A.   Shining Light Parents we interviewed are serving as Affiliate Leaders and / or Caring Listeners. (You can learn more about these resources via menu items at the top of the home page for HelpingParentsHeal.org.) They are deeply honored to help others as they were helped earlier in their journeys.

B.   The parents 'just knew' when it was time for them to help others. Most described it as like 'a calling' that helps them as much as it does others.

C.   In most cases, these parents want to make their children proud of them and create more meaning to their lives. This is a powerful way to optimally heal and transform: look beyond your own suffering and do what you can to assist others. Different cultures have recognized that you get back ten-fold – or more – when you help others. As *The Beatles* put it: "And in the end, the love you take is equal to the love you make."

4. How have you learned to optimally sense your children's living presence?

A.   Many parents smiled and sat up straighter when I asked this question. I could tell it was a source of comfort and peace as they relayed how their children let them know they're still around. They described the process of better sensing their kids as a two-way street; parents need to do their part by being good receivers and transmitters.

B. Parents reported various ways they knew their kids are still alive and well: highly evidential medium sessions (#6); electronic aberrations such as lights and TVs flicking on and off; coins and feathers appearing seemingly out of nowhere; and unusual behavior by birds, insects, and pets. (#28) The variety of signs reflects how very intelligent, creative, and loving the children are.

C. Some parents had difficulty sensing their children. In my experience, this is often due to lower-energy emotions such as guilt, sadness, and anger that can hamper perception of loved ones who have transitioned from earth. Centering practices (#77), breathing techniques (#70), prayer (#89), and meditation (#51) can often help. Another cause of not perceiving your children is having preconceived notions about how they will come through. Being open to when and how that happens helps you be more relaxed and trusting – higher energy emotions that facilitate contact. (#9)

5. What are three things you've learned that you want to share with other parents?

A. Responses to this question ranged widely but were all heart-warming. As with question 4, it was obvious that parents were happy to share their insights. They had all experienced shock, crying, having their world blown apart, and trauma. As a result, they understand what other parents are going through and share wisdom that can only come from surviving it.

B. Common messages included: Your children are still alive. You will see them again. They are happy and whole again. Look for subtle signs and messages that they are very near. Talk to them as though they are present, because they probably are. Tell stories, laugh, cry, invite them to gatherings, and continue to make them part of your family.

C. Parents emphasized that how and when your children transitioned is not your fault. There is a rhythm and wisdom throughout the cosmos that limited brains can't comprehend but open hearts can. They stressed that, no matter how tough your life is right now, you can get through this just as they did. They are here to help so please don't suffer in silence. HPH has so many resources and so many wonderful people who can help you survive and, hard as it may be to imagine, eventually thrive.

6. What is your belief about there being a meaning and timing to your children's passing?

This was the most emotional question of all. Degrees of certainty among parents ranged from 'I really don't know. How can there be?' to 'Absolutely! There is a perfect meaning and timing to how and when they changed worlds.'

Granted, from a limited earthly perspective, the bodily death of children seems totally tragic, senseless, and cruel. However, their answers to this question suggest that there may be more timing and meaning than most people have considered. Opening your hearts and minds, even a little bit, to this possibility can be immensely comforting and healing.

A. As mentioned above in 1(C), parents told beautiful stories about how much their children blessed others. Often, parents didn't know the breadth and depth of this until weeks, months, or even years later. I repeat this point because it's such an important one: your children, even though they lived a short time on earth, may have helped more people than octogenarians who live relatively uneventful lives.

B. Numerous parents shared that they suspected that their children wouldn't live that long on earth. Sometimes it was a feeling or a gentle telepathic voice that let them know. Parents described looking into their children's eyes and feeling they were in the presence of 'an old soul'. Their children seemed to have an otherworldly focus, as though they could see more deeply and profoundly than the average human. Parents hoped their precognitions weren't true, but later found out they were.

Sometimes children *told their parents* they wouldn't be on earth for long. For example, a five-year-old told his mom that he would have to leave her at age 18. The mom assumed it was anxiety about leaving for college, but accidental bodily death did occur at that age.

Other events also provided advanced warnings. One little girl saw angels frequently and they were a big part of her life. However, as this little one advanced in grade school, she didn't talk about them anymore. Nearly thirty years later, however, the daughter said: "Mom, remember how I saw angels when I was little? Well, they're back again." Two weeks later, she passed on in her sleep due to – *from an earthly perspective* – a rare and undiagnosed health problem. However, from a greater reality viewpoint, was it 'just time' for her to rejoin her angels and shine brightly elsewhere?

No matter how these signs came in, these Shining Light Parents considered them to be Divine Grace that prepared them at least somewhat.

C. Many of their stories supported the belief that how and when children pass on involves timing and meaning. Just before their bodies perished in an auto accident or were murdered, children said things like: 'I hope you know how much I love you. I will never leave you. I've been so lucky to have you as my parent'. Sons, who usually weren't emotionally demonstrative with their dads, stood right in front of them and touched their faces while saying this. These heartfelt communications were seemingly 'out of the blue' and deeply intense for no apparent reason.

D. Other events suggest that the souls involved knew they were close to returning Home. Children who previously had no interest in religion or spirituality suddenly asked about God and the afterlife. Others, who had some knowledge about the big picture of life, suddenly wanted to talk about it much more. Some expressed concern about dying when there was no illness or reason for them to be worried. The children crossed over soon after all these events.

E. The most touching statements were made by parents who felt deep gratitude for the privilege of parenting such a special soul for even a short time. They realized their 'children' are really much more than that. This is, in my opinion, one of the highest-level reactions a parent can have. If you're not there yet, set an intention to feel more gratitude and even pride for being selected to support an evolved soul who visited earth for a brief while.

We hope and pray that this book helps you shine ever more brightly. You and your loved ones deserve to be happy, healthy, and fulfilled. What's more, *the world needs your greatest gifts*. After working with many parents, I believe that a 'meta-blessing' from children passing on is this: the tremendous amount of pain and suffering that parents experience can be transmuted into magnificent levels of love, wisdom, and service. Based on everything I know, it's quite likely that your children are participating in a cosmic plan to lovingly help more people:

- *Know and show* who they are, why they're here, and Who walks beside them.

- Enjoy the greatest life that their higher selves have envisioned.

- Serve and bless others in extraordinary ways.

- Help make our world a better place.

Are you ready to work with your children and make this a reality? (#119)

Consider this very inspirational story that was told by a Shining Light Parent at an HPH meeting where I was a guest speaker. While holding *a beautiful crystal*, parents told stories about their children who had graduated from earth-school. Sandra shared that both of her children had moved on. Several people in the group spontaneously said, 'Oh my God. I am so sorry'. Sandra quickly interrupted and said, 'Thank you, but it's OK. I know it was the perfect way and timing for both of them to return Home. And they both are in regular contact.'

Then she gave this stellar example that informs and empowers me as I hope it will you. The most recent contact, she shared, happened when she was getting into bed. Sandra heard her daughter's voice say, "Mom, can you see me?" Sandra replied, "I can hear you, but I can't see you." Her daughter replied, "Mom, *you need to get bigger eyes*!" Other parents gasped, as did I, at the power and wisdom of this statement. It was 'short and sweet' as communications from higher realms often are. It reminded us all to *open our hearts, minds, and eyes*; internalize the messages in this book; and shine brightly in every moment.

Love and light (is all that really exists),

Mark

Appendix A: Becoming Part of HPH

by Nancy Hejna

Members of Helping Parents Heal agree that the organization is a lifeline for them and the people they help. Learning *how* these Shining Light Parents found HPH is very interesting. This appendix shares their answers to the questions: 'How did you find Helping Parents Heal?' and 'What led you to serve?' Many of their answers are similar so we share just some of them.

Finding Helping Parents Heal

"When my kids transitioned, I said out loud while crying and screaming: 'I will search for you and I will find you – whatever it takes.' That night, I looked through YouTube about life after life. I found the documentary 'Mom, Can You Hear Me?' by Craig McMahon. Then I found Suzanne Giesemann, Elizabeth Boisson, wonderful Helping Parents Heal parents, and the mediums in this documentary. When the credits appeared, I was ready with a pen and paper. I joined Helping Parents Heal the next day; it has lifted me." — Ana M, mother of Frankie & JoseLuis

Truc-Co and **Tom** found HPH through a podcast that spontaneously started playing in the car. "On a day shortly after Ailee transitioned, instead of playing the news, Siri popped up on the screen of my car with *We Don't Die* – the podcast by Sandra Champlain. I had never listened to a podcast on my phone or in my car before. It went to a very specific recording: the interview with Elizabeth from HPH! There was an instant connection when we joined in person."

Sandra recalls her search, "It was one of those sleepless nights after Josh passed. I sat at the computer and searched for something that would help me. I really wanted to talk to another parent. That's when I found Helping Parents Heal."

Candy had hundreds of books about the afterlife, but felt she needed one more. "I found Mary Bertrun's book, *The 21 Day Doorway Across the Veil – How to Connect with your Child* and thought 'That's the book I need'. Mary recommended HPH. I finally had found my people, my spiritual tribe."

David: "After Ginger passed on in 1999, I was a member and chapter leader of *The Compassionate Friends*. After Tracy passed, I watched the movie *Life After Life: Mom, Can You Hear Me?* I saw credits about HPH and got on their website. I wanted to join a local group, but there wasn't one. So I called and offered to start one."

Amy B watched the same video. "While watching the video, I jumped up and down and thought, 'These are my people! At last, I found a group.' So I joined right away."

Chris R's wife found HPH by looking at different websites, reading different books, and going to different forums. "She told me about the father's group about a month into our journey." **Jeff H** says his wife also played a major role: "She did a lot of the research. I took the typical man approach: I'll be fine, I'll put a tough face on. But that doesn't work."

Mike says that after his son Dylan transitioned from earth, "I was intellectualizing my grief. I launched into research about the afterlife, out-of-body experiences, near death experiences, astral travel, mediumship, and more. Then I went to a group medium reading with Kat Bailee and Dylan came in. She told me about HPH. I contacted Elizabeth, told her about my idea for an online group for dads, and Helping Fathers Heal was born.

Emma found HPH on YouTube. "I was following the breadcrumbs from my daughter."

Heather followed Dr. Mark Pitstick and Suzanne Giesemann on YouTube. "They gave me an incredible amount of hope and both mentioned HPH."

Mary D spotted Elizabeth Boisson on a podcast. "About a month after Lea passed, I started looking for online support groups. I found Irene Weinberg's *Grief to Rebirth* where Elizabeth was a guest speaker. I listened to her talk with a beautiful smile and laughter. So I looked into HPH and I found a connection with all of it."

Lisa A recalls: "I started delving into information from others who think like me, who know our children still exist. I watched videos from HPH and the energy was there – just as if it was a live experience instead of a recording."

Margaret shares, "After Kenny passed, I was waiting to pass on too but, somehow, this HPH event with Susanne Wilson came up on my Facebook feed. It was held at a place not too far from me. I had never seen a medium but thought I'd go. I was looking for a seat and heard, 'Margaret'. I looked around and saw Lisa Wilcoxson; her son Anthony was good friends with my son. Susanne started talking, but I wasn't paying attention. Lisa realized that Susanne was talking about my son Kenny. That was my first experience with HPH. Every other group I'd been to talked about 'moving on', but in HPH we don't have to leave our kids behind."

Terri: "I had a spiritual awakening when Rick passed, and all these things were happening so fast. I studied mediumship with Christine Salter; parents in her group mentioned HPH, so I joined."

Janean shares, "I grew up in a religion that was not okay with seeking communication with the afterlife. Six months after Sean transitioned, I decided that I couldn't worry about that so I Googled a medium. She had a one-day conference but there were no openings. I was on the waiting list and sarcastically said to the air, 'Okay Sean, if I'm supposed to do this, get me in.' A few minutes later, I got a phone call that someone had cancelled. I had no idea what I was walking into. I saw people from HPH there with so much joy on their faces. I couldn't figure it out and thought, 'I'll never be like that.' But I was so drawn to them that, for several months, I drove two hours to meetings until I started a local group."

Lynn recalls: "I met Mark and Susie Ireland within a month after Devon's body was found. They became our lifeline. They invited us to a party and a woman there was like an angel; it was Elizabeth. There was so much laughter and joy at our table. We loved talking about our kids, and said 'Do you think anybody else has any idea what our common denominator is?'"

Tammy shares, "I met Jeff Olsen and we became friends. He was going to speak at Helping Parents Heal. He said I should check out the group and think about being an Affiliate Leader. I thought it would be a good place to find my tribe."

Hearing about HPH through a family member or friend is common. **Joanna** had a very supportive friend mention HPH. **Ana E** says: "My best friend's sister-in-law is the manager of the funeral home that picked up Alessandro's body and she told me about HPH." **Dolores** shares, "My cousin's cousin reached out to say, 'I'm in this group called Helping Parents Heal and I think it'd be a great idea for you.' HPH focuses on the afterlife and I needed that."

Some parents believe they were led to HPH by their kids. **Jeff H** says: "I refer to our son Devon as the Puppet Master and believe he put the right people in our path. When a friend found out that Devon was missing, she called the medium Deborah Martin and asked if there was anything she could do. Deborah reached out and became a life preserver. She got us in touch with the early founders of HPH."

Sophia: "After Xander transitioned, I heard him say, 'shining light' and repeat it. I looked up that term and found 'Shining Light Parents' which led me to 'Helping Parents Heal'. Then he said, 'Go to their Facebook group'. He continued to guide me even though I argued about the whole thing."

Explains **Megan**, "I met somebody who introduced me to someone they had just met. That person said to go to this support meeting for people whose children had transitioned. I walked in knowing nobody; they started talking about feeling their children in the afterlife. I knew that Lane hadn't gone anywhere; he was with me. I cried for 10 minutes because I was so full of joy that this was a possibility. I know Lane was getting me from person to person so I could find HPH."

"After seven months, I was just kind of guided," **Paola** shares. "I felt that Nicolas' physical body was gone, but his presence was still with us because we received a lot of signs. One day I decided to look at Facebook; the first post I saw was about Elizabeth and HPH."

Christine tells her story: "In 2017, Sara Ruble told me about Helping Parents Heal. There was not a local group here yet, but I attended their conference in 2018. I felt so welcomed and enveloped in love by all of the Shining Light Parents there. It felt like home and I knew that's what I needed."

So many of the parents interviewed found out about HPH through Suzanne Giesemann that the book team nicknamed her 'The Connector'. Here are a few examples...

Carre: "After Grant passed on, I Googled what to call myself because I didn't know the term. Survivors are called widows, widowers, orphans – and then there's 'bereaved parent'. I didn't feel that worked for me. Then I came across a post by Suzanne Giesemann that called us Shining Light Parents."

Tava: "I met Suzanne Giesemann two months after Christina passed. She called me on Mother's Day and told me that the whispers I was hearing were my daughter's voice and that I should talk back to her. That was just mind-blowing. She told me about Helping Parents Heal and that they had an in-person group near me. At the second meeting, Dr. Mark Pitstick spoke. Sometimes you hear exactly what you need to hear right when you need to hear it. I needed the left-brain stuff and every word he spoke was just pouring love into my soul. It was so life changing."

"Back in the mid-nineties, the way we all dealt with grief was very different," **Michelle** says. "I was part of a support group that was incredibly depressing. Then I watched a video of Suzanne Giesemann and she mentioned Helping Parents Heal."

Some parents were attracted to HPH because of similar worldviews about death and the afterlife. **Patti** says, "I had been in other grief groups but didn't feel I could really be myself and talk about the miraculous things that were happening with Adam. I just wanted to shout, 'Oh my gosh, my son is still here!' I couldn't do that in other groups; so when I found HPH, it was like coming home."

Merle prayed and prayed for guidance. "I returned to my Swedenborg spiritual upbringing. My faith taught me that heaven is right here and that heaven is a state of mind. I went back to a Swedenborg YouTube channel (*Off The Left Eye*) and in one of their podcasts they mentioned HPH. I learned from many of their films, books and podcasts. It all reconfirmed what I had always been taught."

Cathy recalls, "I read about Marla, a HPH leader in Tampa with three children who passed on. I couldn't even believe it! Then I read the group mission which was right up my alley. I told everybody in my other grief support group and think I brought nine people with me."

Andy shares, "HPH is the most effective way for me to process my grief. Being with other dads – talking, crying, swearing, laughing – is the most healing thing I've ever done."

Lin shares her story that summarizes the beliefs of many HPH parents. "I was only a few weeks into this journey after Ryan passed and attended another grief group. The first woman I met said, 'Hello, my son died 14 years ago, and it never gets any better'. I was horrified. *In that instant,* I decided that would not be me. They were stuck on telling their story over and over; I left feeling worse than when I arrived. I searched for other groups and found HPH."

The Call to Service

"HPH is like a big tsunami; we've gotten amazing signs and connections with our children, and they go out in

waves to the world. To be part of that is a privilege. As an Affiliate Leader, I don't really do anything, I just hold space for people. Their children do it all."
— Patti, Adam's mom

Devon's mom **Lynn** says, "I'm a Caring Listener. A strong point is that I'm a good listener. I'm calm and like to hear about the parent's journey with their child. I think I bring hope and the possibility of joy into another parent's life."

Lisa L, Amber's mom, states: "After a child's passing, sometimes you feel like you're burdening people with your story and bringing them down. Someone said, 'If I can't talk to you about my child, that's all I need to know about you.' That stuck with me. Sometimes people just need to talk, tell their story, and cry to get it out. I'm there to listen."

"One of my greatest strengths is my ability to listen to people and see myself in them," explains **Megan** who is Lane's mom. "I think this really allows me to connect deeply to people and I get so much out of the experience. As an Affiliate Leader we give, but I get back so much."

Anni relates: "Soon after Anthony transitioned, I wrote to coroners, funeral directors, and other service providers about HPH. I asked them to pass it on to parents with a child who transitioned. I try to raise awareness that our children live on in spirit. It's so hopeful. It's important to come from that vulnerable place and knowing you're able to recover from it. I'm a certified counselor and coach, an author and a shaman."

Louise says: "I'm a nurse so compassion and healing are just part of who I am. There are so many people who have experienced a child's passing in the area where I live. The funeral director is my daughter Jillian's godmother and they have me on speed dial. When a kid dies in the community, she calls me to reach out and I do. I tell them that parents in the HPH group are the most amazing people you'll ever hope to meet."

Jeff shares: "Dads in our Helping Fathers Heal group were all messes at some point. We couldn't speak and would ugly-cry every day. That's okay. You'll find a tab for Helping Father's Heal on Facebook and the HPH website. We meet virtually every Wednesday night and have 30 to 40 dads join in. It's a fabulous brotherhood and judgment-free zone. There's crying, wailing, gnashing of teeth, a few bits of colorful language from time to time."

Margaret saw a specific need after her son Kenny passed and filled the gap. "I started the HPH 'Single Parents Hopeful Hearts' group because there was a big difference about how I was going through this journey compared to my friends who had husbands. I felt like I didn't have support. I had to do everything by myself. I didn't get that hug at night when I was breaking down. Our group also supports grandmothers who are taking care of grandchildren on their own because their son or daughter has passed. We are not a dating group, as some people think by the title, but I'm very good at connecting people and bringing them together."

Explains Davey's mom **Allison**. "I'll have a parent tell me, 'I just can't connect with my child. I don't know how. I know they're still with me, but...' I'll say, 'What would your child tell you about what you're saying right now?' The parent responds, 'He'd say 'Mom, lighten up, you're being silly.'' Then I'll say, 'You just connected with your child;

you shared his personality, his spirit, conveyed it to me. You connected.' It's that simple."

"I wanted to pay it forward as soon as I noticed I wasn't crying every day," explains **Amy**. I've been given the most beautiful gift from my child that is real. I decided to become an Affiliate Leader to help others understand your connection is real and you can survive what some consider unsurvivable."

Maggie, Mitch's mom, adds: "I felt like I was in a place in my healing journey where I was ready to give back. I was ready to help others know that we can heal our grief. We can find peace, joy and love if we do the necessary work of confronting our emotions and learning how to navigate through them. I was inspired to become an Affiliate Leader."

Carol relates: "With all the signs that Kyle was bombarding us with – not just me, but his whole family – I got almost giddy. It changed everything. There really is an afterlife! Our kids are still here, and other parents need to know that. I wanted to spread the great news and help lessen the suffering."

Susan and **Bill V** felt guided to serve others by their son Greg: "Bill was meditating, as he does a lot to connect with our son, and Greg came to him. Bill asked, 'How can I help? How can I give back?' Greg said, 'Start the Calgary chapter of Helping Parents Heal.'"

Ana M, mother of Frankie and JoseLuis, underscores the importance of HPH as an international service organization. "It's wonderful to serve others because you get to interact with so many other parents who are on the same journey. You know you're not alone and your children are also there. It's all online. We have parents from all over the world: Spain, South America, Australia, Central America, Europe, Mexico, and the United States."

"You feel guided by the kids," **Terri**, mom of Rick, says. "I began to feel quite intuitive as to what was needed. Sometimes it was to have a chat room just to open up a place for parents to come in and share space. Sometimes it will be to bring in an HPH provider to lead in meditation, or a medium. I was passionate about bringing this to the UK."

Paola shares: "Three years after Nicolas passed on, I felt that I was in a place of peace. I was able to support other parents and share my story. I felt compelled." **Conrado** agrees: "As I progressed, I felt it was almost my duty to try to help other people along the same path, to show them that there is a way out."

Mary D strives to honor her daughter. "I feel my motivation comes from Lea. Even prior to her diagnosis, it was always about serving others and gratitude. That's how she lived her life. When she was sick and couldn't work anymore, she still offered her marketing skills to entrepreneurs and small businesses in the community. Serving and giving back is a way to shine brighter for my daughter and for myself."

Lin, Ryan's mom, shares, "Before I started our HPH group, I had attended other grief groups. One had us sit in a circle and talk only about death and sadness. They would pass around a heavy rock, and whoever held the rock would speak. I knew this was not good energy and thought 'Surely we can do better.' No heavy rocks for HPH groups!"

Scott's mom **Sara** says: "When Elizabeth asked if I wanted to do a group about soul planning, I said 'Oh, absolutely!' When I read

Robert Schwartz's book, *Your Soul's Plan*, it opened my world up to something that just made so much sense. In my group we talk about soul plans and how our connection with our children is so extraordinary when you really start looking."

"I'm motivated to help people understand that life is eternal; that we are going through one phase of life here on earth right now and our next stage of life will be the afterlife," Sam's mom **Kerry** says. "I try to gently have those discussions to assure people that their children are not gone; they are in another space, and communication with them is very possible. If parents can be mindful of a difference in energy around them – like cold, heat, or vibration – don't dismiss it. Communication between earth and beyond is so subtle that it's easily missed."

Chandra helped establish a HPH group in India after her son Naman changed worlds. "We wanted to do this because India has such a variety of spiritual beliefs. There is nothing at all like HPH in India because there is a lot of stigma around bereavement. People don't talk about death and loss openly. We are honored to share kinship and bring empathy and understanding."

"Elizabeth contacted me about eight months after Derek transitioned and I happily agreed to become a Caring Listener," explains **Lisa.** I also lead the group 'Children Who Have Passed from Substance Use' that meets the first Thursday of every month. We focus on positive things – signs from our kids and hopeful messages."

Cindy shares: "When I set up our HPH group, I wanted to go within and think about what would work. I ask Josh, my son in spirit, before every meeting and get downloads about what to discuss. Too often in life, we try to *go around* painful things. The only thing you can do with grief is *go right through the center of it* and recognize 'you are not your grief'. Think of grief as the landscape – trees, grass, and houses – while the road you're on is your path."

Appendix B: Tributes to Parents and Children

by Nancy Hejna

"The morning Davey transitioned I was extremely worried about him. He'd gone for a run, came back, hugged me tightly and put his face against mine. He was 24 years old. I just remember the roughness of his skin. He said, 'Dad don't worry, I will never leave you.' Hearing that three hours before he passed is something I reflect on every day, even now." — David A, Caring Listener and leader of HPH Meditation group

Kudos to the Shining Light Parents who participated in these interviews. And, of course, special thanks to their postmaterial children who are living in realms characterized by peace, joy, love, and light. Their brightness comes through each of their parents. They are connected to us by an unbreakable bond of love across dimensions.

This chapter contains answers to the question: 'Please tell us about your child's life and passing.' We are honored to know a glimpse about their lives, transition to the next phase of life, and continuing legacy.

Note: For clarity, the parent(s) are listed first, then their child / children in parentheses.

Allison and David A (Davey) Our son Davey transitioned in July of 2016 from a single-vehicle car accident. I didn't really focus on that and never even went out to see the site. I was focused on finding him.

Amy B (McKellar) My 19 year-old son McKellar ended his earthly experience six and a half years ago on July 1st.

Amy D (Chris) Chris was our beautiful 21-year-old son. He had just graduated from college and was living at home with us while he was looking for a job. He was killed in a kind of a random accident that happened very suddenly.

Amy S (Brandon) My son Brandon crossed over in March 2020 — essentially just as the world shut down. He passed from accidental Fentanyl poisoning.

Ana E (Alessandro) My son Alessandro was born premature and lost his hearing. Everybody loved Alessandro; he was charming, special, and had a twisted sense of humor. Once he started college, however, he was struggling. He was self-medicating and I decided he should come back home. He told me he was going out with his friends for one last hurrah. On my way to pick him up, I got a call that they found Alessandro dead at the bottom of a cliff. No one has come forward to tell us what happened.

Ana M (Frankie and JoseLuis) Frankie and JoseLuis were very significant to me. I'm a mother of four boys: Frankie and JoseLuis were the sons who were always with me, checking up on me, and calling me. Frankie was murdered, and JoseLuis transitioned from an accidental drug overdose.

Andrea (Chloe) I call my daughter Miss Chloe because she had all this attitude and it comes through even now. She transitioned in February 2016 from cancer.

Andy B (Joshua) Joshua was born on Saint Patrick's Day in 1999 and was my firstborn. He came into the world in an emergency, and he left it in a car accident in September 2019. I say that his soul was outside his body before he ever touched the tree. Even though it was incredibly painful for me, I'm glad there was no suffering. He went out the way that he wanted – doing something he loved. After four years, I can now say that without absolutely losing my mind and crying.

Andy and Kathy (Aiden and Conor) We had a 'normal life' for a long time: three children, a dog, and great jobs. In March of 2013, our youngest son Aiden, who was 15, transitioned by suicide. We never saw it coming; it was a huge awakening. Eight months later, our oldest son Conor, who was 20, transitioned in an accident while he was away at college.

Angela B (Emily and Erin) I have two children in spirit. Over 25 years ago, Emily transitioned at 34 weeks of age. A year later, Erin Hope was born. Erin was fit and healthy, but on her 22nd birthday, she was in bed with a sore stomach which turned out to be cancer. At that time, she couldn't be admitted to the hospital because of Covid.

Angela and Danny L (Ethan) "Our beautiful 18-year-old boy Ethan passed on from a motor vehicle accident in December 2019. This was absolutely devastating for our family. He fell asleep driving, had a head-on collision with a semi-trailer, and passed instantly. He had a beautiful heart and wonderful sense of humor. Quite often, I still hear his laugh in my head.

Ann G (Matthew and Scott) Our sons Matthew and Scott both transitioned in the spring of 2020. Matt passed at age 30 from an accidental overdose. He had been clean for three years and was working really hard, recently engaged, and going back to school. Matt was – and still is – really smart, funny, creative, and musical. My stepson Scott passed on two months later. Scott struggled with mental health and also addiction to numb the pain and cope. His lungs failed, but there was never a clear diagnosis. So they both had struggles on this earth.

Anna and Frode (Alexander)

Anna: Alexander was supposed to be born in March 2004, but he didn't come out until mid-April. He was late into this world, but once he got here he was always in a hurry. He was a very active kid, very curious, and always eager to explore. He was kind, supportive, had a lot of friends, and a wonderful ability to make people laugh.

Frode: In May 2020 at age 16 while driving a moped, he was involved in a traffic accident caused by the police. He transitioned at the scene. To honor his memory, his friends arranged a caravan of mopeds that attracted hundreds of teenagers. The event has been repeated every year; that has meant the world to us and given us strength.

Anne-marie (Harry) My boy Harry was 19 and had a fatal motorbike accident in October 2020. He loved working on cars and motorbikes and was an apprentice carpenter. He was on his pathway to being a very successful young man. At his funeral, his employer said that he was the best worker they'd ever had.

Anni (Anthony) Anthony is forever 43. He transitioned by suicide in 2022; I kind of knew that day. I knew from when he was born that he wasn't going to stay for a long time.

Annie and Marc (Zenzi) Zenzi was an amazing drummer, gifted, had natural rhythm, and knew the lyrics of songs. Zenzi transitioned in

March 2018 from complications of leukemia that was diagnosed only four days before passing when we were on a family vacation in Salt Lake City. I just figured it was a higher altitude and easier exit.

Antonietta (Daniel) My son Daniel was a fun-loving kid and a jokester. He always took time to play with little kids and animals. I knew he was an old soul. He had a curiosity and the things he said were so profound. Daniel had melanoma, which is rare in kids, and transitioned at the age of 16 four years ago. He did not want to leave us, but cancer did not give him a choice.

Babette (Daniel) My Daniel was born in May 1991. When he was in middle school, he experienced anxiety and depression and began to self-medicate with pot. Daniel had a wonderful group of friends, but at age 25 he had an overdose and that's how he passed on.

Barb (Jordan) Jordan is my middle child, a wonderful spirit and he was a fantastic kid growing up. He transitioned at the age of 25 about two months before finishing his PhD in nuclear physics. We did not see that coming; he was in pain and we didn't know it. We went through analyzing that and the guilt that goes along with it.

Beth N (Steven and Erin) My story starts in 1997 when my brilliant son Steven was five years old. He was diagnosed with a very aggressive form of pediatric cancer. He went through treatment for two and a half years before he passed on. Several years later, we moved to the Seattle area. Erin was starting high school and struggled with her mental health; she never could get over the loss of her brother. She sometimes asked for help, but really didn't want it – she thought she could do it on her own. She went away to college and wanted to be a social worker to help kids like herself.

But after a breakup with a boyfriend, she left this world by suicide. She was just lonely.

Beth and Rick O (Jessica and Joshua) Our children passed in 1999 when Jessica was nine and Josh was seven. A drunk driver going over 80 miles an hour ran a red light and broadsided our minivan. Both kids passed on within 30 minutes but we somehow survived. Looking back, we understand that our kids came here to help us get into a position to be able to help other people. They continue to help us from the other side with that.

Beverly (Mason) My son Mason is our oldest child and was born in 1999. When he was a senior in high school, he got sick with bone cancer. He transitioned at age nineteen a little less than two years after being diagnosed. It's been five years, but it seems like it just happened yesterday.

Bill and Susan V (Gregory) Our son Gregory passed on nine years ago in 2014 from the effects of drug abuse. He did not overdose; that's what many people think of when they hear that. He passed from cannabinoid hyperemesis syndrome, a very rare disorder that affects those who are chronic or heavy users of marijuana.

Candi (James) James transitioned in April of 2021 by suicide. I know it was hard for him to stay here and his soul wanted to go home.

Candy (Amber) My daughter Amber was 43 years old and she had just come home from work as a doula. She went across the street to say hello to the neighbor and was shot. She was an innocent bystander.

Carol A (Tyler) My beautiful son Tyler crossed to the other side at 19 years old in 2015 when he was on a motorcycle.

Carol K (Kyle) From the start, I just knew Kyle was different and an amazing kid. Kyle is so bright, inquisitive, creative, and became a footwear designer. He had mental health struggles and the Covid thing was too much for him. Of course, he wasn't alone; I learned that about 93,000 people in the U.S. passed on from overdoses that year.

Carolyn (Cara) Cara was 16 years old when she was in a car accident in January 2020. She was an amazing child: a gifted athlete, a kind person, and loved the outdoors. Cara let me know that she was around very shortly after transitioning. I started Googling NDEs – I was like 'Oh I think there's an afterlife'. I knew about heaven but never thought about it.

Carre (Grant) My son Grant was an extremely bright light while he was here in the physical, and is an even brighter light in spirit. He was a friend to everyone. He had an accident a couple of days before his twelfth birthday.

Cathy (Ross) Ross had addiction issues for about nine years prior to his passing. He was bright and played guitar, but had a real struggle. He was funny as heck and a real leader among his friends. He gave the best hugs.

Chandra (Naman) My son Naman is a wonderful kid. I'm using *is* very deliberately because I believe he is in the present. He changed worlds in September 2018. Naman left home in the middle of the night; we thought that was very unlikely for a kid who loved his home. We later found out that he passed on the same day by drowning after jumping from a bridge into a creek.

Chris M (Paige) Paige was born in November 1994. She was the most focused, driven, smart, and competitive person I ever knew. At nine, she was diagnosed with a genetic disorder that gradually took her mobility away. By sixth grade, she lost her ability to walk unassisted but Paige was determined to do what she wanted to do. She got into college and graduated with a degree in systems biology. She wanted to be a genetic counselor or in public health. At age 22, she fell out of her chair and had a cardiac arrest while fighting to get up.

Chris R (Sean) Sean Gabriel was born in September 1997 and passed on nearly 24 years later. He was found unconscious at his home and had taken what he thought was ketamine. Sean was in the ICU on life support; three days later, we had to make the decision that no parent wants to make.

Chris V (Daniel) Daniel transitioned on July 4, 2020 by his own hand. He loved everyone and was the least judgmental person I have ever known. He had a big heart and a special fondness for animals and children. He was definitely an empath and felt everybody else's feelings very deeply.

Christiane (David) David is my only son. My husband passed on when he was six and David took on the role of being the man of the house. He was diagnosed with osteosarcoma just before he turned 14, and passed six years ago in 2017 at the age of 18.

Christine (Andrew) Andrew was just a fun-loving kid. He always had this perpetual impish grin on his face that would kind of make you wonder what he was up to next. On the evening before his high school graduation party, Andrew decided to go to a local concert with a couple of friends. I got the call that is every parent's worst nightmare: the boys had been in a car crash caused by a drunk driver who hit them from behind on the highway. We had to make that devastating decision to take him off life support. We went from planning a high school graduation party to planning a funeral in the blink of an eye.

Cindy (Josh) The words I think of for Josh are inventor and visionary. As he grew older, he created videos and wrote stories that always had an unusual depth. The biggest thing I remember is his big heart, empathy, and aura. He just wanted to help people.

Claudia A (Emma) Emma was a happy and healthy child. As she grew up, she was very kind; above all, she was a provincial gymnast. That was her passion. She had done gymnastics since she was three years old. She was competing, but at age 12 she was diagnosed with bone cancer and had her leg amputated. The cancer came back when she was 15.

Colleen (Denis) Denis was and still is a bright light. He made everybody laugh, was most empathetic, and just wanted everybody to be happy. Denis was a funny guy! He got sick in August of 2019. His lungs just didn't cooperate and they couldn't be fixed.

Conrado and Paola (Nicolas) My son Nicolas would just light up the room when he walked in. An ISIS-inspired terrorist used a truck as a weapon of mass destruction. He jumped the curb, and he ran over 86 people. My son was one of the victims.

Craig (Alexander) My son Alexander was adopted from Ukraine at the age of six months. He was diagnosed with autism, was nonverbal, and dependent on us for his physical needs. Alexander passed from a seizure when he was 16 years old.

Danny (see Angela and Danny)

David A (see Allison and David)

David D (Genevieve and Tracy) I have two daughters in spirit. Ginger was my first loss. Her actual name was Genevieve, but she went by Ginger, which she chose herself. She passed at the age of 20 in a car accident. My eldest daughter Tracy crossed over from a very rare form of bile-duct cancer at the age of 42. She left behind three young boys. So I've had both kinds of loss: the instant tragic kind, and watching your child transition over an extended period of time from cancer.

Deb (Dean) Dean was 24 when he transitioned by suicide in 2020. He was on the autism spectrum and struggled with anxiety and social things, but he was very high functioning.

Dolores (Eric) One of my favorite things about Eric is that he was a drummer. Going to gigs where his band played were some of the most joyful times of my life. He was a caring and compassionate young man. Soon after college when he got his first 'real' job, he said: "I'm going off to dinner with my new co-workers because I want to get to know them." He didn't come home that night. He had been in a solo car accident; we never understood why he veered off the road. Afterward, I was angry, but I didn't lose my faith. I prayed to understand what was going on. Over time I believe that prayer was answered.

Emma (Jesse) My daughter Jesse transitioned on the 12th of the 12th month in 2021. I've had signs about that date. She may have contributed to her passing; they don't believe she meant to, it was partly accidental. She was studying physics, but decided to follow her passion of drama, acting, and musical theater.

Elizabeth (Chelsea and Morgan) My daughter Chelsea didn't live long, only two days. Morgan was two when Chelsea passed. He was this enormous bright light in any room that he entered. He had the best bear hugs. He was always an advocate for the weak. He passed near the base camp of Mount Everest while on a college exchange program.

Frode (see Anna and Frode)

Galen (Weston) My husband Brian and I have two sons. Our older son Weston passed on in August 2018 quite suddenly from complications of an unexpected seizure. He was otherwise a very healthy, strong, happy, and gregarious 32-year-old entrepreneur running his own transportation company.

Heather H (Xavier) My son Xavier Alexander was born to us in February 2020. He crossed over at five months of age from SIDS.

Heather S (Luke) Luke was 20 years old when he transitioned in 2022. Luke chose to leave this world by suicide. He loved, and he still does love, basketball, music, our family, and nature and animals.

Irene (Carly) My daughter Carly Elizabeth came into this world screaming; she was full of life, vibrant, a great kid. She passed in 2013 from cancer.

Janean (Sean) Sean was larger than life and the instigator of all adventures in our family. He attended college at the University of Arizona. He volunteered for the Big Brother - Big Sister program and he took underprivileged kids on camping trips. He was a hiker, athletic, on the Dean's List, and had a million friends. Then he had a brief period of psychosis for about 18 months; we don't know where it came from. I believe he self-medicated with marijuana and that caused some of the psychosis. At some point, he realized his brain wasn't okay. He wasn't willing to stick around in that kind of pain, so at age 22, he took himself to the other side.

Jayme (Devon) Devon was an avid sports fan, played baseball and football, and was skilled at everything. He was an Eagle Scout, a good friend, a good boy. He had a wonderful sense of humor and I still feel him trying to make me laugh. Devon told me once that he felt awkward, as if he didn't really fit into this world. He ended this earthly experience in September 2021 at the age of 24. It took us totally off guard. Devon has since told me it was an impulsive decision, but it doesn't matter how he passed. He's still with us.

Jean (Joseph) Joseph was on his way to visit one of his girlfriends and had a car accident. That resulted in major surgery; unfortunately, when the pain medicine stopped, he started finding his own. Two years after that, he transitioned in a single-person car accident. I miss his physical presence, his beautiful blue eyes, his laugh, and how he would light up a room any time he walked in. The energy just lifted.

Jeff C (Austin) Austin, our first born, was born November 29, 1995. He passed on a couple of weeks after his 24th birthday of hypothermia. He was kind, fun-loving, caring, intelligent.

Jeff H and Lynn (Devon) Our son Devon passed in Frankfurt, Germany in November of 2009. We don't really know exactly what happened, but we think he fell victim to some folks who didn't have his best interests at heart. He went missing a few days before Thanksgiving and his body was found a few days before Christmas, which kind of screwed up the holidays for us for years. He was 22.

Joanna (Peter) My son Peter was born on Christmas day. He passed on at age 22 several days after his car hit a tree. He'd gone out late at night and was driving too fast and lost control. He was an amazing drummer and was playing with 11 bands of different genres. All those other drummers played his drums for his funeral. We've stayed in touch.

Joyce (Holly and Michelle) Holly was born in September 1972 and passed at the age of two from a seizure disorder, failure to thrive, and other syndromes. We knew after she was born that her life with us would be short; even so, the grief was still overwhelming. My daughter Michelle was murdered by an ex-boyfriend at the age of 42. The call in the middle of the night was devastating. In her lifetime she was a scholar, a writer, an artist, witty, and thoroughly devoted to her profession.

Judith (Carly) My niece Carly passed at age 24 in February of 2013. She became the ringleader on the other side too: she led her mom Irene to HPH. That's how I became involved, through my sister Irene.

Kate (Warren) My son Warren was born in July 2001 and was a really active, joyful, bouncy little boy. We used to call him Tigger because he just bounced everywhere. He passed on in February of 2019 by suicide. Almost as soon as he transitioned, he showed up in the light so I didn't have to search for him. I immediately got into mental health and suicide prevention advocacy. I know he is doing the work with me and we are a great team.

Kathy (see Andy and Kathy)

Kaylene (Alex) My son Alex was 14 years old when he 'went Home' as I like to call it. He just went to sleep and didn't wake up.

Kelley (Aleia Jade) Aleia Jade transitioned in May 2022 via suicide. She was a connector. If you were in a room with her, she would lock eyes with people just to make sure that they knew that someone 'saw' them.

Kerry (Sam) I'm the mother of Sam, who passed as a 19-year-old in a car accident 12 years ago. He was always a loving child and very popular with adults and children. He had a huge friendship base and was very mature for someone so young. There were a thousand people at his memorial service. He was so much fun and still continues to be; I very much feel his presence. I only discovered my mediumistic abilities after Sam's passing.

Laurie (Garrett) My son Garrett was a handful from the moment he was born. In hindsight, he lived a huge life during his 19 years on earth. He loved his family, animals, the thrill of competition, and had a great sense of humor. I still hear him from the other side and his sense of humor is still there. He got into some drugs when he was about 18 years old. We tried many things to help him but, with no notice, he left earth on 11/11/2010. He was a loving son, a great kid, and he just left.

Lin (Ryan) My son Ryan was 26 when he passed in February 2019. He was very empathetic and was coming into his own. Ryan graduated from Michigan State University and had a job helping disadvantaged kids and coaching football. Football was his love. Unfortunately he made a bad decision in taking a Xanax that was laced with Fentanyl. Ryan passed from an accidental Fentanyl poisoning on my couch.

Linda O (David) My son David was 28 years old when he transitioned to spirit by suicide. Everything was going well for him: he had a job he loved and a beautiful girlfriend expecting their first child. But he suddenly became physically unwell; this massively impacted his mental health and he became depressed. Within a month, he passed on. It was a massive shock.

Linda R (Chris) My son Chris was 36. We don't know the date of his passing because his body was never found. He has been back in spirit many times to various people – not just to me – to say that it was not suicide. It was just an accident.

Lisa A (Derek) My son Derek, I call him Derry, was a free spirit. He was a no-shirt, no-shoes, and often a no-job kind of child. He loved to surf, skateboard, play drums, fish, and be outdoors. He was always up for the next adventure. He transitioned at 20 years in September 2020 from a substance.

Lisa H (Shayne) My boy Shayne was born in January of 2004. He was just a sparkling ray of light; his smile lit up a room as did his energy – so much exuberance and vitality. Shayne transitioned in January 2020, one week after his 16th birthday.

Lisa L (Amber) My daughter Amber was 25 when she passed after suffering from an eating disorder since the age of 14. Amber had so much success in life and was such an exuberant person. She was an old soul, witty, and funny.

Lisa W (Michael and Anthony) Michael ascended in 2000 at age 12. He was a special needs child who didn't speak or walk and he was G-tube fed. He got pneumonia suddenly one weekend and was gone within two days. Anthony was a freshman at Arizona State University; he had been at a party and had a toxic reaction to a poisonous chemical. He crossed into spirit in April of 2013.

Louis (Joe) Joe was born deaf in 1990. He was smart, and very active in youth groups in church and school. He also had a difficult side, which led to a lot of adventures. In December 2010, Joe entered the next life by suicide.

Louise (Jillian) Jillian lived fully and was here for a good time, not a long time. She was very intuitive — an old soul. She was killed instantly at the age of 19 in a car accident.

Lynn (see Jeff H and Lynn)

Mabel (Leo) My son Leo is my only child. He was and still is incredible. He was 19 years old when he passed from bacterial meningitis.

Maggie (Mitch) Mitch was 27 years old when he transitioned after an accidental overdose of opioids. I like to talk more about him versus the story around his addiction. He was loving and friendly and personable. He would help anybody that needed help.

Marc (see Annie and Marc)

Margaret (Kenny) Kenny was my first-born child and seemed very different. I'd have him in his little baby seat and he'd be looking up and laughing. He really saw things and felt things. Early on, I realized how lucky I was to be his mom. Kenny transitioned in October 2004 at age 23 after a motorcycle accident. Many mediums have told me he was out of his body before impact so he didn't suffer.

Marie (Sienna) Sienna was a very artistic and creative child. I always used to call her an old soul because she had this understanding about life that even challenged my own views. She passed when she was 11 from an Arteriovenous Malformation in her brain that suddenly dissected. So it was a very sudden and tragic passing.

Marla (Shane, Nicole, and Ryan) I'm always a little bit hesitant to talk about my three of five children passing because it feels overwhelming to people. But that's just been my life.

Mary B (Chaz) Chaz was a young Marine who left by his own hand. No one expected it, certainly not us.

Mary D (Lea) Lea was the youngest of my two children and she was 32 years old when she left this world. She passed of sepsis and colorectal cancer.

Mary Y (Katherine) My daughter Katherine passed on at age 29. She was on life support for five days; we made the decision to take her off because they gave us no hope of recovery.

Megan (Lane) Lane was a force of light for sure. He had a great sense of humor and loved to break the tension with a joke. He was always good at getting everybody laughing or out of a bad mood, which was awesome. He struggled a lot with substance abuse which I believed was self-medication for his mental health issues. At age 20, he moved to Hawaii to start a new life. While there, he had some beautiful experiences including getting married and having a daughter. But four days after his 23rd birthday, he passed on by suicide.

Merilene (Kevin) Kevin was born in 1997. He was very handsome and active – a loving kid and wonderful son. Unfortunately, he was diagnosed with cancer in 2014. After three and a half years of struggle, he transitioned in June 2018.

Merle (Chris) Chris was a huge personality: loud, caring, had the best smile, and empathy for people like I've never seen. He gave everybody the biggest and the best hugs. He made some really poor choices when he was a teenager and had to take responsibility for that. That taught our whole family a lot; we learned to live one day at a time. Chris loved his two boys and partner of six years. He transitioned at age 34 from a cerebral aneurysm.

Michelle J (Ben and Grace) I had three children and two of them are in spirit. My baby son Ben was born by emergency caesarean and was a little premature. The doctors thought he was going to be fine, but sadly he took a turn for the worse and passed on when he was five hours old. My daughter Grace was born a year later and was the most delightful, gorgeous, and funny little kid. She was involved in a terrible car accident at 19 while driving.

Michelle T (Jordan) Jordan was the most beautiful, loving, and sweet girl. In 2016, she developed gastroparesis which paralyzes the stomach and the intestinal tract. She ate food but it wouldn't stay down so she was in the hospital a lot. She passed at age 23.

Mike (Dylan) Dylan was very charismatic, good looking, intelligent, and an accomplished percussionist. He was born in October 1992 and crossed over at Thanksgiving in 2016 from addiction. For some of these kids, life is just really tough. I think he had just burned himself out so he chose his exit point.

Nancy (Will and Joey) My oldest son Will transitioned in 2016 at the age of 26 of an accidental heroin overdose. Two years later in 2018, my youngest son Joey, a wonderful six-foot-three ball of energy, passed in car accident on the day of his oldest sister's wedding.

Paige (Jaimie and Brian) My baby girl Jaimie passed on January 1, 1989; she was stillborn and that was really hard. My son Brian was three at the time. After that, I had two more miscarriages. Although my heart was broken again and again, I was so grateful that I still had Brian. Then, 15 years ago at the age of 23, Brian was murdered.

Pamela (Michele) My daughter Michele passed in 2018 when she was just two weeks shy of her 21st birthday.

Paola (see Conrado and Paola)

Pat (Tyler) My son Tyler... I feel like he's a shining light kid. When I think of him, it just makes me smile. He transitioned in October 2013; he was 20 years old and it was due to an overdose.

Patricia (Melissa) Melissa passed suddenly at 18 years old. She was like the mayor of our town. Everyone knew her.

Patti (Adam) My son Adam was 17 when he left this world in a tragic car accident. Adam is my youngest and my adventurer. We always joked that we would have had more kids, but having Adam was like having 10 kids. He had so much energy and was so much fun and so present in our lives.

Ramona (Mia) Mia was born in January 2020 and passed on in February 2020. She was here on earth just for a month. She suffered from a genetic syndrome that was incompatible with life. She lived her brief life in hospital and I was there every single day.

Renee (Zack) At the age of 17 months, Zack fell eight feet through a stair railing and had severe brain injury. We were told he would never walk again, but he proved them wrong. He was active, successful, good hearted, and there was nothing that held him back. He crossed over at age 24 after experiencing more things in his life than I have in mine.

Rhonda (Reese) Reese transitioned from earth in March 2017; he chose to pass.

Rick (see Beth and Rick)

Rosanne (Lee) My 30-year-old son Lee and his dog passed in January of 2018 by accidental carbon monoxide poisoning. It's common for children who pass at a younger age to have a sense of urgency about them – as though their soul knows they're not going to be on earth very long. Lee was like that.

Sandra (Josh) Josh was 30 years old. He was very bright and one of the friendliest, kindest people I've ever known. He passed from an accidental overdose of fentanyl.

Sara (Scott) Scott was an amazing and brilliant child who was in college studying environmental sciences. He was so passionate about everything he did. He was working at a national park in Colorado for the summer when I got a message that he passed on in his sleep. Scott had a seizure disorder and took medication for it regularly. He passed from strep throat, dehydration, and elevation. It was like the perfect storm came in and took him away.

Sherry (Gabriel) My baby Gabriel was in this world for a very short time. I like to think of him as my shooting star. I had a miscarriage in 2010; it was the first time I ever experienced grief. I didn't know it would hit me so hard. Almost 14 years later, I'm in a much better place. A lot of healing, clarity, and spiritual seeking has occurred.

Sophia (Xander) Our youngest child Xander transitioned at the age of 14 by suicide. He was our funny little guy, our practical joker, and full of energy. He loved to dance and was just a happy go-lucky little fella. He left us in November of 2019.

Sue (Austin and Kyle) Austin was born premature in 1990 and just lived 14 hours. I didn't really go looking for him because I didn't really know him. Kyle was actually named after him — Kyle Austin. He was born in 1999 and passed in 2019 at age 20.

Susan (see Bill and Susan)

Tammy (Chris) Chris is an absolute joy. He had a herniated disc and became addicted to pain pills. His insurance company wouldn't approve surgery, so they sent him to a pain clinic. They gave him pain medication; he became addicted and overdosed.

Tava (Christina) Christina transitioned in March 2015 after health issues. I choose to focus on her life rather than her death. She lived nearly 18 years of an amazing and brilliant life. I'm so blessed because I got to be the mother of the most amazing human being I've ever known. She's brought me places since her passing that I would have never ever gone.

Terri (Rick) Rick had meningitis when he was three weeks old. He recovered, but out of all my children, Rick was the one I worried about. He was such a cute kid, so funny and giggly, and had such a lovely nature! I felt he was always on the go because he had an anxious energy. As he came into his early teens, the addiction side began to show and escalated the last nine months of his life. He passed from an overdose at the age of 23.

Tom J and Truc-Co (Ailee) Ailee was our youngest child, our miracle baby. She had hepatoblastoma, liver cancer that metastasized to her lungs. She passed just shy of her third birthday during surgery.

Tom M (Kevin) Kevin passed in June of 2018, a month before his 20th birthday, after a 3 1/2 year battle with sarcoma.

Truc-Co (see Tom J and Truc-Co)

Ty (Shayna) My daughter Shayna passed unexpectedly at 15 years old in 2015. It was one of those unexplained deaths, especially for a kid, and was likely an unknown heart condition.

Warren (Nolan) Nolan is a musical kid, he wrote a ton of music. He passed in his sleep, when he had just turned 15, in August of 2020. He had no symptoms, no history of health issues. It's called sudden, unexplained death in childhood, like SIDS.

Wendy (Hugh) Hugh was 20 years old when he passed from Fentanyl poisoning in April 2020. He had been introduced to Percocet at a fraternity party in college and quickly became addicted. Over the span of 10 months, we did absolutely everything to help him. We really thought he had turned a corner and things were looking good. Then this happened. When somebody passes from an accidental overdose, there's a fear that this is how they will be remembered, but he was a million other things.

Appendix C: Resources for Optimal Healing and Transformation

by Mark Pitstick

We hope you regularly use the following resources and share them with others.

Website home page: HelpingParentsHeal.org

Note: there are many resources on this site so please take the time to familiarize yourself. For example, under the Affiliate Groups tab, you'll find resources for siblings, dads, special interest groups, and more.

Caring Listener and Affiliate Leader interviews:
HelpingParentsHeal.org/YouTubeVideosAffiliateLeaderCaringListenerInterviews

Facebook: Facebook.com/Groups/HelpingParentsHeal

Instagram: Instagram.com/HelpingParentsHeal/

YouTube: YouTube.com/c/ElizabethBoissonHPH

Linktree: Linktr.ee/HelpingParentsHeal

HPH Book: Life to Afterlife: Helping Parents Heal, The Book https://www.amazon.com/dp/B09HG2FDZ2

HPH Movie: *Life to Afterlife: Mom, Can You Hear Me?* (Available at Amazon and free on YouTube Youtube.com/watch?v=icwhBSN4rHQ)

Join the Helping Parents Heal Facebook Group to access all the online and in-person events. There is a main group:

www.facebook.com/groups/helpingparentsheal and hundreds of Affiliate Groups available.

Join a Local HPH Group: If there is no local group nearby to attend in-person meetings, you are welcome to join any HPH Affiliate group that offers online meetings. You can even consider starting one if that feels right for you. HelpingParentsHeal.org/AffiliateGroups

Talk with Caring Listeners: This free service is provided by parents who have gone through 'the dark night of the soul' and are now Shining Light Parents. They share what worked for them, listen with care, and suggest resources. HelpingParentsHeal.org/CaringListeners

Attend Online Meetings: Attend online meetings that are open to all HPH members; one or more HPH webinars are held on weekday evenings. Hear a variety of experts on afterlife, healing, and contacting your children. HelpingParentsHeal.org/Calendar

Watch Interviews with Affiliate Leaders and Caring Listeners: These parents share so much hope, inspiration, and practical steps for healing and transforming that it's listed twice! HelpingParentsHeal.org/YouTubeVideosAffiliateLeaderCaringListenerInterviews

Read Articles at SoulProof.com/Articles to answer your biggest questions and provide holistic solutions for your toughest challenges. Most helpful for HPH members have been:

> #1 Scientific Evidence That Bodily Death Is NOT the End of Life
>
> #2 When Children Change Worlds
>
> #4 When a Loved One Passes On by Suicide

Listen to Interviews with top experts about life and afterlife: guests interviewed include Wayne Dyer, Raymond Moody, Anita Moorjani, Brian Weiss, Michael Newton, Caroline Myss, Gary Schwartz, and other luminaries. One of the questions often asked was, "What do you say to parents with children who passed on?"

SoulProof.com/Radio

Use Experiential Sessions from HPH classes:

1. Holistic Breathing Technique (#70) Start with this as directed for one month to release lower energies and emotions such as anger, hopelessness, guilt, and more. To access this video, visit: www.youtube.com/watch?v=Fu4b3tLnu8s

2. Ask Your Soul, Angels, and G.O.D. (#71) Add this session and continue (7a) as recommended. This one helps you access guidance and assistance from your higher self, your spiritual support team, and The Light. You can optimally heal, transform, serve others, and create more meaning to your child's life.
www.youtube.com/watch?v=MTXJLt4FlgU

3. Facilitated Afterlife Contact (#9) After a month of using #1 and two months of #2, you should feel more peaceful and clear. At that point, you'll be more likely to sense your child's living presence using this technique. www.youtube.com/watch?v=ZHmMcbxVt48

4. Pre-Birth Planning (#25) This session allows you to explore whether your higher self may have chosen *the possibility* of adversity including the bodily death of your child. If so, what were your goals for planning that? How can you fulfill those and create more meaning from *what appears to be* – from a limited human perspective – a senseless tragedy?
www.youtube.com/watch?v=BYfnwTbVPPU

Get Personalized Answers and Holistic Solutions: As long as my schedule allows, I will email brief but informative and resource-packed replies to parents, siblings, and other close family members member *at no charge*. Email me at mark@soulproof.com with *your biggest questions and toughest challenges*.

Note: My inexpensive audio products, books, and documentary film can help you optimally heal, transform, and discover silver linings to your child's bodily death. *If you cannot afford them,* email me at mark@soulproof.com and we'll send complimentary digital products.

This is a lot of information, so please start with one or two resources, then add more as you feel led to do so. Over time, these steps can help you immensely, as it did this mom:

"I discovered your life-transforming work through HPH and know it was divinely guided. I continue to delve into your generous body of teachings and am practically buzzing with each insight. Thank you for expanding my awareness of who I and my daughter really are, and teaching about the greater reality."

About the Author

Mark Pitstick, MA, DC, has over fifty years of experience helping people in hospitals, pastoral counseling settings, mental health centers, and holistic health care clinics. His training includes pre-med undergrad, theological school, masters in clinical psychology, doctorate in chiropractic health care, and postgrad clinical nutrition studies. He also provided suicide prevention counseling while in theology school and that has remained a priority outreach.

When Mark was six years old, he told his parents that a beautiful sunset 'reminds me of God.' At age 10, he became aware of situational 'clair' abilities, and has had numerous revelatory and spiritually transformative experiences. After working with many dying and suffering persons in hospitals, he was motivated to find evidence-based answers to existential questions: 'Who am I? Why am I here? What happens after I die? Will I see my departed loved ones again? Is there really a God? If so, why is there so much suffering? How can I best live during this brief earthly experience?'

Dr. Pitstick has written eight books to help people deeply know and show that their time on earth is a totally safe, meaningful, and magnificent adventure amidst eternity. His ten audio products use deep relaxation, breathing techniques, and guided imagery so more people *realize and demonstrate* they are integral, infinite, eternal, and beloved parts of Source.

Mark produced the *Soul Proof* documentary film with interviews of people who had near-death experiences, afterlife contacts, and other spiritual encounters. He hosted two radio shows, *Soul-utions* and *Ask the Soul Doctors,* with interviews of top experts in consciousness studies and soulful living. Mark has worked closely with Helping Parents Heal **for over ten years. He** provides clinical support for Affiliate Group Leaders and Caring Listeners, writes a Q & A for their newsletters, and provides regular webinars.

Dr. Pitstick directs the SoulPhone Foundation, a non-profit organization that: (1.) teaches the collective evidence for life after death, and (2.) supports postmaterial communication technology R & D at the University of Arizona. He is a research assistant for the SoulPhone Project; data from years of research have now *definitively demonstrated scientifically* that life continues after bodily death. The project seeks to create communication technology with postmaterial persons (the so-called 'deceased'). This project meets criteria for true scientific research: controlled, double-blinded, replicated, randomized order, multicentered, and published in peer-reviewed scientific journals.

To learn more, visit SoulProof.com and SoulPhone.org.

Note: If you need but cannot afford any book or audio session, email mark@soulproof.com and we will send free digital products.

Made in the USA
Monee, IL
22 July 2024